Study Guide for

Discovering Computers
2007

A GATEWAY TO INFORMATION

Web Enhanced — COMPLETE

Gary B. Shelly
Thomas J. Cashman
Dave Nuscher

THOMSON
COURSE TECHNOLOGY

COURSE TECHNOLOGY
25 THOMSON PLACE
BOSTON MA 02210

SHELLY
CASHMAN
SERIES.

Australia • Canada • Denmark • Japan • Mexico • New Zealand • Philippines • Puerto Rico • Singapore
South Africa • Spain • United Kingdom • United States

THOMSON

COURSE TECHNOLOGY

Study Guide for
Discovering Computers 2007:
A Gateway to Information, Web Enhanced
Complete

Gary B. Shelly
Thomas J. Cashman
Dave Nuscher

Managing Editor:
Alexandra Arnold

Associate Product Manager:
Heather Hawkins

Editorial Assistant:
Klenda Martinez

Production Editor:
Pre-Press Company, Inc.

Cover Image:
Pre-Press Company, Inc.

Compositor:
Pre-Press Company, Inc.

Printer:
Globus

ISBN-13: 978-1-4188-4371-7
ISBN 1-4188-4371-7

DISCOVERING COMPUTERS 2007
A GATEWAY TO INFORMATION
WEB ENHANCED
STUDY GUIDE

CONTENTS

PREFACE

This Study Guide is intended as a supplement to *Discovering Computers 2007: A Gateway to Information, Web Enhanced* by Gary Shelly, Thomas Cashman, and Misty Vermaat. A variety of learning activities are provided in a format that is easy to follow and helps students recall, review, and master introductory computer concepts. Each chapter in the Study Guide includes:

- A **Chapter Overview** summarizing the chapter's content that helps students recollect the general character of the concepts presented.
- **Chapter Objectives** specifying the goals students should have achieved after finishing the chapter.
- A **Chapter Outline** designed to be completed by the students, helping them to identify, organize, and recognize the relationships between important concepts.
- A **Self Test** that reviews the material in the chapter through Matching, True/False, Multiple Choice, Fill in the Blank, and Complete the Table questions.
- **Things to Think About**, which consists of questions formulated to help students develop a deeper understanding of the information in the chapter.
- A **Puzzle** that provides an entertaining approach to reviewing important terms and concepts.
- **Self Test Answers** and a **Puzzle Answer** that students can use to assess their mastery of the subject matter.

In addition to the activities in each chapter, the Study Guide also offers a **To the Student** section that provides tips on using the textbook effectively, attending class, preparing for and taking tests, and using this Study Guide.

TO THE STUDENT

Would you like to be promised success in this course? Your textbook, *Discovering Computers 2007: A Gateway to Information*, can be a source of the knowledge you need to succeed. Unfortunately, no textbook alone can guarantee understanding of the subject matter; genuine understanding depends to a great extent on how hard you are willing to work. Other available resources, however, can *help* you to get the most out of this course. That is the intent of this Study Guide.

What follows are tips on using the textbook, attending class, preparing for and taking tests, and utilizing this Study Guide. Most of the tips in the first three areas not only will help to improve your performance in this course, they also can be applied to many of your other college classes. The tips in the last area are designed to explain how this Study Guide can enhance your mastery of the material in *Discovering Computers 2007: A Gateway to Information*.

Using the Textbook

The textbook is one of your most important tools for building a solid foundation in the subject matter. To use your textbook most effectively, follow these guidelines:

Survey the whole text first. The table of contents supplies an overview of the topics covered. The preface explains the textbook's objectives and features. Notice how chapters are organized, the way key terms and concepts are indicated, how illustrations and tables are used, and the types of exercises that conclude each chapter. Look for special features interspersed throughout the book and use the index to clarify information.

Start by skimming the chapter. Read the chapter introduction, which gives you an idea of the chapter's relevance, and study the chapter objectives, which indicate what you are expected to learn. Next, browse the chapter. Look at the section headings to get a feeling for how sections are related to each other. Note bold text – these terms are important. **Primary Terms** are shown in bold black characters and include terms commonly used in the computer industry and in advertisements, or terms that identify a major category. *Secondary Terms* are shown in bold blue-gray italicized characters and include terms primarily used by IT professionals and other technical people, terms that identify subcategories, or terms that are discussed in more depth in a later chapter. Finally, read the Chapter Summary at the end of the chapter. The summary restates, in broad terms, the major concepts and conclusions offered in the chapter.

Carefully read the entire chapter. Some instructors prefer that you only skim a chapter before class, and then do a detailed reading after their lecture. Other instructors want you to read the chapter thoroughly before class. When you read through the text, make sure you understand all of the key terms and concepts. Pay particular attention to illustrations (photographs, diagrams, and tables) and their captions; often, they can help clarify ideas in the text. Examine the boxed write-ups interspersed throughout the chapter (At Issue, FAQ, Looking Ahead, Career Corner, Quiz Yourself) and use the Web Links in the margins to obtain additional information. Write in your book: highlight important points, note relationships, and jot questions. Carefully examine the review material (Chapter Review) and list of important words (Key Terms). If there is anything you do not remember or understand, go back and re-read the relevant sections. Do the exercises that deal specifically with the content of the chapter (Checkpoint). Finally, complete any additional exercises (Learn It Online, Learn How To, or Web Research) that your instructor may assign.

♤ Attending Class

Attending class is a key ingredient to success in a course. Simply showing up, however, is not enough. To get the most out of class, follow these guidelines:

Arrive early and prepared. Sit close enough to the front of the room to hear well and clearly see any visual materials, such as slides or transparencies. Have any necessary supplies, such as a notebook and writing implement or a notebook computer, and your textbook. Be ready to start when your instructor begins.

Take notes. For most people, taking notes is essential to later recall the material presented in class. Note-taking styles vary: some people simply jot down key words and concepts, while others prefer to write more detailed accounts. The important thing is that the style you adopt works for you. If, when you later consult your notes, you find they do little to help you remember the subject of the lecture, perhaps you should try to be more comprehensive. On the other hand, if you find that in taking notes you frequently fall behind your instructor, try to be briefer. Review your notes as soon as possible after class.

Do not hesitate to ask questions. Often, people are afraid to ask questions because they think they will appear foolish. In reality, asking good questions is a sign of intelligence; after all, you have to be insightful enough to realize something is unclear. Keep in mind that frequently your classmates have the same questions you do. Good questions not only help to clarify difficult topics; they also increase the depth of your understanding by suggesting relationships between ideas or establishing the significance of concepts. Learn the best time to ask questions. In small classes, sometimes it is possible to ask questions during instruction. In a larger setting, it may be best to approach your instructor after class or to make an appointment. If you feel really lost, your instructor may be able to recommend a peer tutor or an academic counseling service to help you.

⌖ Preparing for and Taking Tests

Tests are an opportunity for you to demonstrate how much you have learned. Some strategies are certain to improve performance on tests. To do your best on a test, follow these guidelines:

Find out as much as you can about the test. Ask your instructor what material will be covered, what types of questions will be used, how much time you will have, and what supplies you will need (pencil or pen, paper or bluebook, perhaps even notes or a textbook if it is an open-book test). You will be more likely to do your best work if there are no surprises. Occasionally, copies of previous tests are available from the department or school library. These are invaluable aids in test preparation.

Use your resources wisely. Start studying by reviewing your notes and, in *Discovering Computers 2007: A Gateway to Information*, the Chapter Review section at the end of each chapter. Review carefully and attempt to anticipate some of the questions that may be asked. Re-read the sections in your textbook on topics you are not sure of or that seem especially important. Try to really comprehend, and not merely memorize, the material. If you truly understand a concept, you will be able to answer any question, no matter what type or how it is worded. Understanding often makes remembering easier, too; for example, if you know that an ink-jet printer works by spraying dots of ink on a page, it is simple to recall that ink-jet printer resolution is measured in dots per inch (dpi). When memorizing is necessary, use whatever technique works (memory tricks, verbal repetition, flash cards, and so on).

Avoid cramming. To prepare for an athletic contest, you would not practice for twelve straight hours before the event. In the same way, you should not expect to do well on a test by spending the entire night before it cramming. When you cram, facts become easily confused, and anything you do keep straight probably will be remembered only for a short time. It also is difficult to recognize how concepts are related, which can be an important factor in successful test taking. Try to study in increments over a period of time. Use the night before the test to do a general review of the pertinent material, concentrating on what seems most difficult. Then, get a good night's sleep so you are well-rested and at your best when it is time for the test.

Take time to look through the test. Arrive early enough at the test site to get properly settled. Listen for any special instructions that might be given. Skim the entire test before you start. Read the directions carefully; you may not have to answer every question, or you may be asked to answer questions in a certain way. Determine the worth of each part, the parts you think can be done most quickly, and the parts you believe will take the longest to complete. Use your assessment to budget your time.

Answer the questions you are sure of first. As you work through the test, read each question carefully and answer the easier ones first. If you are not certain of an answer, skip that question for now. This guarantees that you get the maximum number of "sure" points and reduces worry about time when later dealing with the more difficult questions. Occasionally, you will find that the information you needed to answer one of the questions you skipped can be found elsewhere in the test. Other times, you will suddenly remember what you need to answer a question you skipped as you are dealing with another part of the test.

Use common sense. Most questions have logical answers. While these answers often require specific knowledge of the subject matter, sometimes it is possible to determine a correct answer with a general understanding and a little common sense. As you work through a test, and when you go back over the test after you are finished, make sure all your answers are reasonable. Do not change an answer, however, unless you are sure your first answer was wrong. If incorrect answers are not penalized any more than having no answer at all, it is better to try a logical guess than to leave an answer blank. But, if you are penalized for incorrect answers (for example, if your final score is the number of correct answers minus the number of incorrect answers), you will have to decide whether or not to answer a question based on how confident you are of your guess.

✐ Using this Study Guide

The purpose of this Study Guide is to further your understanding of the concepts presented in *Discovering Computers 2007: A Gateway to Information*. Each Study Guide chapter should be completed *after* you have finished the corresponding chapter in the book. The Study Guide chapters are divided into sections, each of which has a specific purpose:

Chapter Overview This is a brief summary of the chapter's content. The Chapter Overview helps you recall the general nature of the information in the chapter.

Chapter Objectives This is a list of the same objectives that introduce the chapter in the book. After completing the chapter, review the Chapter Objectives to determine how many of them you have met. If you have not reached an objective, go back and review the appropriate material or your notes.

Chapter Outline This is a partially completed outline of the chapter with page numbers where topics can be found. The Chapter Outline is designed to help you review the material and to assist you in organizing and seeing the relationships between concepts. Complete the outline in as much depth as you feel necessary. There is no one "right answer" in the Chapter Outline. Because your completions should be meaningful to *you*, they may be different from a classmate's. You can refer directly to the text as you work through the outline while re-reading the chapter, or you can fill in the outline on your own and then use the text to check the information you have supplied.

Self Test This is a tool you can use to evaluate your mastery of the chapter. The Self Test consists of five different types of questions: matching, true/false, multiple choice, fill in the blanks, and complete the table. Take the Self Test without referring to your textbook or notes. Leave any answer you are unsure of blank or, if you prefer, guess at the answer but indicate you were unsure by placing a question mark (?) after your response. When you have finished, check your work against the Self Test Answers at the end of the Study Guide chapter. Each answer is accompanied by the page number in *Discovering Computers 2007: A Gateway to Information* where the answer can be found. Review any solution that was incorrect or any reply that was uncertain.

Things to Think About These questions are meant to help you better grasp the information in each chapter. Because specific answers to the Things to Think About questions will vary, no solutions are given. The true purpose of these questions is to get you to contemplate the "why" behind concepts, thus encouraging you to gain a greater understanding of the ideas, their connections, and their significance.

Puzzle This activity is designed to review important terms in an entertaining fashion. The Puzzle in each chapter is one of four types: a word search puzzle, a crossword puzzle, a puzzle in which words must be placed in a grid, or a puzzle involving words written in code. Every puzzle offers definitions or descriptions and asks you to supply the associated term. The solution to each puzzle is given.

DISCOVERING COMPUTERS 2007
STUDY GUIDE

CHAPTER 1
Introduction to Computers

Chapter Overview

This chapter introduces basic computer concepts such as what a computer is, how it works, and what its advantages and disadvantages are. You also learn about the components of a computer. Next, the chapter discusses networks, the Internet, and computer software. The many different categories of computers, computer users, and computer applications in society also are presented. This chapter is an overview. Many of the terms and concepts introduced are discussed further in later chapters.

Chapter Objectives

After completing this chapter, you should be able to:

- Recognize the importance of computer literacy
- Define the term *computer*
- Identify the components of a computer
- Discuss the advantages and disadvantages of using computers
- Recognize the purpose of a network
- Discuss the uses of the Internet and World Wide Web

- Distinguish between system software and application software
- Describe the categories of computers
- Identify the elements of an information system
- Describe the various types of computer users
- Discuss various computer applications in society

Chapter Outline

I. A world of computers [p. 4]

Computer literacy entails _____

_____

II. What is a computer? [p. 6]

A computer is _____

_____

_____

A. Data and information [p. 6]
- Data is _____

  _____

- Information is _____

  _____

An FAQ helps you _____

_____

B. Information processing cycle [p. 6]

Computers process _____ (input) into _____ (output).

Instructions are _____

The information processing cycle is _____

_____

III. The components of a computer [p. 7]

Hardware is _____

_____

A. Input devices [p. 7]

An input device is _____

_____

Widely used input devices: _____

_____

B. Output devices [p. 8]

An output device is _____

_____

Common output devices: _____

C. System unit [p. 8]

The system unit is _____

_____

The system unit circuitry usually is part of or is connected to the motherboard.

Two main components on the motherboard are the processor and memory.

- The processor (CPU) is _____

  _____

- Memory is _____

  _____

D. Storage devices [p. 8]

Storage media contain _____

A storage device records and retrieves _____

Common storage devices: _____

E. Communications devices [p. 9]
Communications devices enable_____

Communications devices: _____

IV. Advantages and disadvantages of using computers [p. 9]
A user is _____

A. Advantages of using computers [p. 10]
Speed: _____
Reliability: _____
Consistency: _____
The phrase garbage in, garbage out points out _____

Storage: _____
Communications: _____

B. Disadvantages of using computers [p. 10]
Violation of privacy: _____
Impact on labor force: _____
Health risks: _____
Impact on environment: _____

V. Networks and the Internet [p. 11]
A network is _____

A computer is online when _____

Networks allow the sharing of resources such as: _____

A. The Internet [p. 12]

The Internet is _____

_____

People use the Internet to _____

_____

The Web contains _____

_____

A Web page contains _____

_____

To publish a Web site means _____

_____

A photo sharing community is _____

_____

A blog is _____

_____

A podcast is _____

_____

VI. Computer software [p. 15]

Software, also called a program, is _____

_____

A graphical user interface (GUI) is _____

_____

An icon is _____

_____

The two types of software are system software and application software.

A. System software [p. 15]

System software consists of _____

_____

Two types of system software are the operating system and utility programs.

1. Operating system [p. 15]

An operating system is _____

_____

2. Utility programs [p. 16]

A utility program is _____

_____

B. Application software [p. 16]

Application software consists of _____

_____

Popular application software includes _____

_____

C. Installing and running programs [p. 17]

Installing is the process of _____

_____

To run software means _____

_____

To load software means _____

_____

To execute a program means _____

_____

D. Software development [p. 18]

A programmer (or developer) is _____

_____

VII. Categories of computers [p. 18]

Computer categories are based on size, speed, processing power, and price.

The seven major categories of computers are:

- _____
- _____
- _____
- _____

- _____
- _____
- _____

VIII. Personal computers [p. 19]

A personal computer is _____

_____

PC-compatible refers to _____

_____

Two popular series of personal computers are the PC and the Apple.

Major categories of personal computers:

A. Desktop computers [p. 20]

A desktop computer is _____

_____

A tower model has _____

The gaming desktop computer offers _____

A Media Center PC is _____

IX. Mobile computers and mobile devices [p. 20]

A mobile computer is _____

A mobile device is _____

A. Notebook computers [p. 20]

A notebook computer (or laptop computer) is _____

1. Tablet PC [p. 21]

A Tablet PC is _____

A digital pen is _____

B. Mobile devices [p. 21]

Some mobile devices are Internet-enabled, which means _____

1. Handheld computer [p. 21]

An ultra personal computer (uPC) or handtop computer is _____

A stylus is _____

2. PDA [p. 22]

A PDA (personal digital assistant) is _____

3. Smart phone [p. 22]

A smart phone is _____

Convergence has led to _____

X. Game consoles [p. 22]

A game console is _____

_____

XI. Servers [p. 23]

A server is _____

_____

XII. Mainframes [p. 23]

A mainframe is _____

_____

XIII. Supercomputers [p. 23]

A supercomputer is _____

_____

XIV. Embedded computers [p. 24]

An embedded computer is _____

_____

Some everyday products that contain embedded computers include:

- _____   - _____
- _____   - _____
- _____

XV. Elements of an information system [p. 25]

An information system is composed of _____

_____

For an information system to be successful, all of these elements must be present
and work together.

XVI. Examples of computer usage [p. 26]

Different categories of users rely on computers for a variety of purposes.

A. Home user [p. 26]

A home user is _____

_____

_____

B. Small office/home office user [p. 28]

A small office/home office (SOHO) includes _____

_____

_____

_____

E-commerce is _____

_____

A Web cam is _____

_____

C. Mobile user [p. 29]

A mobile user is _____

_____

_____

_____

D. Power user [p. 29]

A power user requires _____

_____

Multimedia combines _____

_____

E. Large business user [p. 30]

A large business user is _____

_____

_____

_____

Enterprise computing is _____

_____

The function of the information technology (IT) department is _____

_____

A kiosk is _____

_____

Telecommuting is _____

_____

F. Putting it all together [p. 31]

Figure 1-35 on page 31 summarizes the requirements of each category

XVII. Computer applications in society [p. 32]

A.   Education [p. 32]

_____

_____

_____

_____

B. Finance [p. 32]

_____

_____

_____

_____

Online banking is _____

_____

Online investing is _____

_____

C. Government [p. 33]

_____

_____

_____

_____

D. Health care [p. 34]

_____

_____

_____

_____

Telemedicine is _____

_____

E. Science [p. 34]

_____

_____

_____

_____

A neural network is _____

_____

F.   Publishing [p. 35]

_____

_____

_____

_____

G.   Travel [p. 36]

_____

_____

_____

_____

H.   Industry [p. 36]

_____

_____

_____

_____

Computer-aided manufacturing (CAM) is _____

_____

Self Test

Matching

1. ____ input device
2. ____ output device
3. ____ system unit
4. ____ storage device
5. ____ communications device
6. ____ game console
7. ____ utility program
8. ____ installing
9. ____ Internet-enabled
10. ____ supercomputer

a. mobile computing device designed for single-player or multiplayer video games

b. allows a user to enter data and instructions into a computer

c. writes the instructions necessary to process data into information

d. setting up software to work with a computer

e. type of device that can connect to the Internet wirelessly

f. box-like case that contains electronic components of the computer used to process data

g. enables a computer to send data to and receive data from other computers

h. collection of computers connected together via telephone lines, modems, or other means

i. permits a user to perform maintenance-type tasks

j. records and/or retrieves items to and from a medium

k. any component that can convey information to one or more people

l. capable of processing more than 100 trillion instructions in a single second

True/False

____ 1. Through computers, society has instant access to information from all around the globe.

____ 2. Most computers today cannot communicate with other computers.

____ 3. A mouse contains keys that allow you to type letters of the alphabet, numbers, spaces, punctuation marks, and other symbols.

____ 4. Three commonly used input devices are a printer, a monitor, and speakers.

____ 5. Storage differs from memory in that it holds items only temporarily while the processor interprets and executes them, whereas memory can hold items permanently.

_____ 6. A network is a collection of computers and devices connected together via communications devices and transmission media.

_____ 7. More than one billion people around the world use the Internet daily for a variety of reasons.

_____ 8. Application software serves as the interface between the user, the system software, and the computer's hardware.

_____ 9. A computer's size, speed, processing power, and price typically determine the category it best fits.

_____ 10. Few SOHO (small office/home office) computer users communicate with each other through e-mail.

Multiple Choice

_____ 1. How does information differ from data?
  a. information is a collection of raw unprocessed facts
  b. information can include words, numbers, images, and sounds
  c. information is organized, meaningful, and useful
  d. information is processed to produce data

_____ 2. What are examples of input devices?
  a. keyboard and mouse
  b. central processing unit (CPU) and memory
  c. printer and monitor
  d. all of the above

_____ 3. Which of these storage media has the storage capacity for full-length movies?
  a. CD-ROM
  b. DVD-ROM
  c. Zip disk
  d. all of the above

_____ 4. Which of the following is an advantage of using computers?
  a. Computers can perform information processing cycle operations with amazing speed, reliability, and accuracy.
  b. Computers can store huge amounts of data.
  c. Computers can communicate with other computers.
  d. all of the above

_____ 5. Which of the following controls access to the resources on a network?
  a. client
  b. application service provider
  c. server
  d. graphical user interface

_____ 6. Why do people use the Internet?
    a. meet or converse with people around the world
    b. access sources of entertainment and leisure
    c. shop for goods and services
    d. all of the above

_____ 7. Word processing, spreadsheet, database, and presentation graphics software are what type of software?
    a. system software
    b. operating systems
    c. application software
    d. utility programs

_____ 8. What is a workstation?
    a. a large, expensive, very powerful computer that can handle hundreds or thousands of connected users simultaneously
    b. a mainframe computer powerful enough to function as a server on a network
    c. an expensive, powerful desktop computer designed for work that requires intense calculations and graphics capabilities
    d. a popular type of handheld computer that often supports personal information management applications

_____ 9. What is the fastest, most powerful category of computers—and the most expensive?
    a. personal computers
    b. minicomputers
    c. mainframe computers
    d. supercomputers

_____ 10. A local law practice, accounting firm, travel agency, and florist are examples of what type of computer user?
    a. mobile user
    b. small office/home office user
    c. power user
    d. large business user

Fill in the Blanks

1. _____ entails having the knowledge and understanding of computers and their uses.

2. A(n) _____ is someone that communicates with a computer or employs the information it generates.

3. When a computer connects to a network, it is _____.

4. The world's largest network is the _____, a worldwide collection of networks that links together millions of computers.

5. The _____ is a global library of information available to anyone connected to the Internet.

6. A graphical user interface uses visual images such as _____ that represent programs, instructions, or some other object.

7. Some software requires you to insert the program disc into the drive while you use, or _____, the software.

8. In some cases, users access a server via a personal computer or a(n) _____, which is a device with a monitor, keyboard, and memory.

9. A(n) _____ user requires the capabilities of a workstation or other powerful computer.

10. _____ refers to the use of computers to assist with manufacturing processes such as fabrication and assembly.

Complete the Table

CATEGORIES OF COMPUTERS

Category	Physical Size	Number of Simultaneously Connected Users	General Price Range
Personal computers (desktop)	Fits on a desk	_____	_____
_____	Fits on your lap or in your hand	_____	Less than a hundred dollars to several thousand dollars
Game consoles	_____	One to several	_____
_____	_____	Two to thousands	Several hundred to a million dollars
Mainframes	Partial room to a full room of equipment	_____	_____
_____	_____	Hundreds to thousands	$500,000 to several billion dollars
Embedded computers	_____	Usually one	_____

Things to Think About

1. Do the four operations in the information processing cycle (input, process, output, and storage) always have to be performed in order? Why or why not?

2. Why is each component of a computer system (input devices, system unit, output devices, secondary storage devices) important?

3. Why is software the key to productive use of computers?

4. Why is each element of an information system (hardware, software, data, people, and procedures) important?

Puzzle

All of the words described below appear in the puzzle. Words may be either forward or backward, across, up and down, or diagonal. Circle each word as you find it.

```
O Z R Q W G E D P O W E R U K V Y M J Y V O N
K C R F S K E Y G O L N X D M G X T Y G L F Y
R E P I H U C A R M M B R O S S E C O R P J E
O W L P H Y P W F E G A R O T S J Q I H X X R
B S W O Y I Z E H S G E M A R F N I A M E U A
M T U P N I W U R W X K P K F S R C M Q K U W
P A M D N C V O H C R S U G P Z P P Q V B D T
L V C A E W S Z V A O E I Y R V S U Y J H R F
N S X V T H Y Y X L R M M G H K P X Y U Y Q O
H G D D W C S J P X O D P M Y K G O P A M J S
F N C A O V T W N B C Z W U A M J N J F M N K
I O M T R P E W P L T S Z A T R O G L G M J S
N I K A K O M Z C O U M M K R E G O N M T M T
O T T F Z D U G W G O U M S J E R O I Z E E I
C A E D A C N R K U L H I A K X V U R I B J U
I M N B I A I O T T K E W I A G N K D P N M G
B R R Q L S T P I B U D N W T T L B G D G E M
K O E I Q T U M M N P W D L W E W I T E Y M I
G F T F X T E U X A U S E R R H L Y I M Q O A
G N N K Z D U Y R F C G E D K D B B E P Z R T
O I I Y I A X Z L J C B U Q O A I D A C U Y X
P Y B A G F D S I K B M E G I P Y Q N T B B K
V G I N S R T T W Y J K X W N H A N D H E L D
```

Interprets and carries out instructions

Allows interaction using visual images

Worldwide collection of networks

An informal Web site consisting of time-stamped articles in a diary or journal format

Collection of unorganized facts

Electronic and mechanical equipment

Type of user who requires the capabilities of a workstation or other powerful computer

Provides personal organizer functions such as a calendar and appointment book

Type of computer small enough to fit in one hand

Small image that represents a program

Organized, meaningful, useful data

Video camera that displays its output on a Web page

Temporarily holds data and instructions

Combines text, graphics, sound, video, and other elements

Collection of connected computers

People who write computer instructions

Instructions to process data into information

Type of PC; a notebook computer on which you write or draw using a digital pen

Another name for a handtop computer

Recorded audio stored on a Web site that can be downloaded to a computer or digital audio player

Where data is held for future use

Fastest, most powerful computer

Box-like case housing computer circuitry

Communicates with a computer or uses the information it generates

Expensive and powerful desktop computer

Type of hardware component that conveys information to one or more people

Type of hardware component that allows you to enter data or instructions into a computer

Self Test Answers

Matching	True/False	Multiple Choice	Fill in the Blanks
1. *b* [p. 7]	1. *T* [p. 4]	1. *c* [p. 6]	1. *Computer literacy* [p. 5]
2. *k* [p. 8]	2. *F* [p. 6]	2. *a* [p. 7]	2. *user* [p. 9]
3. *f* [p. 8]	3. *F* [p. 7]	3. *b* [p. 9]	3. *online* [p. 11]
4. *j* [p. 8]	4. *F* [p. 8]	4. *d* [p. 10]	4. *Internet* [p. 12]
5. *g* [p. 9]	5. *F* [p. 8]	5. *c* [p. 11]	5. *Web* or *World Wide Web* [p. 12]
6. *a* [p. 22]	6. *T* [p. 11]	6. *d* [p. 12]	6. *icons* [p. 15]
7. *i* [p. 16]	7. *T* [p. 12]	7. *c* [p. 16]	7. *run* [p. 17]
8. *d* [p. 17]	8. *F* [p. 15]	8. *c* [p. 20]	8. *terminal* or *personal computer* [p. 23]
9. *e* [p. 21]	9. *T* [p. 18]	9. *d* [p. 23]	9. *power* [p. 29]
10. *l* [p. 23]	10. *F* [p. 28]	10. *b* [p. 28]	10. *CAM* or *Computer-aided manufacturing* [p. 36]

Complete the Table

CATEGORIES OF COMPUTERS

Category	Physical Size	Number of Simultaneously Connected Users	General Price Range
Personal computers (desktop)	Fits on a desk	*Usually one (can be more if networked)*	*Several hundred to several thousand dollars*
Mobile computers and mobile devices	Fits on your lap or in your hand	*Usually one*	Less than a hundred dollars to several thousand dollars
Game consoles	*Small box or handheld device*	One to several	*Several hundred dollars or less*
Servers	*Small cabinet*	Two to thousands	Several hundred to a million dollars

Mainframes	Partial room to a full room of equipment	*Hundreds to thousands*	*$300,000 to several million dollars*
Supercomputers	*Full room of equipment*	Hundreds to thousands	$500,000 to several billion dollars
Embedded computers	*Miniature*	Usually one	*Embedded in the price of the product*

Things to Think About

Answers will vary.

Puzzle Answer

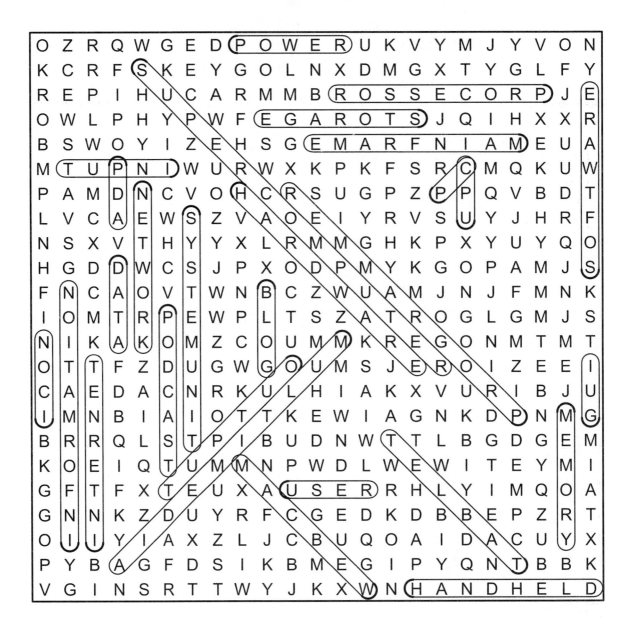

DISCOVERING COMPUTERS 2007
STUDY GUIDE

CHAPTER 2
The Internet and World Wide Web

Chapter Overview

This chapter presents the history and structure of the Internet. It discusses the World Wide Web at length, including topics such as browsing, navigating, searching, Web publishing, and e-commerce. It also introduces other services available on the Internet, such as e-mail, FTP, newsgroups and message boards, chat rooms, instant messaging, and Internet telephony. Finally, the chapter lists rules of netiquette.

Chapter Objectives

After completing this chapter, you should be able to:

- Discuss the history of the Internet
- Explain how to access and connect to the Internet
- Analyze an IP address
- Identify the components of a Web address
- Explain the purpose of a Web browser
- Search for information on the Web
- Describe the types of Web sites

- Recognize how Web pages use graphics, animation, audio, video, virtual reality, and plug-ins
- Identify the steps required for Web publishing
- Describe the types of e-commerce
- Explain how e-mail, FTP, newsgroups and message boards, mailing lists, chat rooms, instant messaging, and Internet telephony work
- Identify the rules of netiquette

Chapter Outline

I. The Internet [p. 68]

The Internet (or the Net) is _____

_____

_____

_____

Users connect to the Internet to _____

_____

_____

II. History of the Internet [p. 69]

Advanced Research Projects Agency (ARPA) was _____

_____

ARPANET was _____

_____

A host is _____

_____

NSFnet was _____

_____

Internet traffic is _____

_____

The World Wide Web Consortium (W3C) is _____

_____

III. How the Internet works [p. 70]

Data sent over the Internet travels via networks and communications media owned and operated by many companies.

A. Connecting to the Internet [p. 70]

Dial-up access takes place when _____

_____

Broadband Internet connections include _____

_____

DSL (digital subscriber line) is _____

_____

A cable modem allows _____

_____

Fixed wireless high-speed Internet connections use _____

_____

A satellite modem communicates with _____

_____

Hot spots provide _____

_____

B. Access providers [p. 71]

An access provider is _____

_____

An ISP (Internet service provider) is _____

_____

Types of ISPs:

- A regional ISP provides _____

_____

- A national ISP provides _____

_____

An online service provider (OSP) offers _____

_____

A point of presence (POP) is _____

_____

A wireless Internet service provider (WISP) is _____

_____

C. How data travels the Internet [p. 72]

Computers connected to the Internet transfer data and information using
servers and clients.

The Internet backbone is _____

_____

D. Internet addresses [p. 73]

An IP (Internet protocol) address is _____

_____

A domain name is _____

A top-level domain abbreviation identifies _____

_____

Dot-com is _____

_____

The Internet Corporation for Assigned Names and Numbers (ICANN) assigns

_____

The domain name system (DNS) is _____

_____

A DNS server translates _____

_____

A DNS server is _____

_____

IV. The World Wide Web [p. 75]

The World Wide Web (WWW), or Web, consists of _____

_____

A Web page is _____

All visitors to a static Web page see _____

A dynamic Web page allows _____

_____

A Web site is _____

A Web server is _____

A. Browsing the Web [p. 75]

A Web browser, or browser, is _____

_____

A home page is _____

A microbrowser is _____

_____

Downloading is _____

_____

B. Web addresses [p. 76]

A URL (Uniform Resource Locator), or Web address, is_____

_____

The http (Hypertext Transfer Protocol) at the start of a Web address is _____

_____

To pull information means _____

To push content means _____

C. Navigating Web pages [p. 77]

A hyperlink, or link, is _____

_____

Surfing the Web means _____

_____

To activate a link, you _____

_____

D. Searching for information on the Web [p. 78]

A subject directory is _____

A search engine is _____

_____

1. Subject directories [p. 78]
    A subject directory provides _____

    _____

2. Search engines [p. 80]
    Search text, or keywords, is _____

    _____

    Hits are _____

    A spider is _____

E. Types of Web sites [p. 82]
    There are eleven basic types of Web pages:
    1. Portal [p. 82]
        A portal offers _____

        _____

        A Web community is _____
        A wireless portal is _____

        _____

    2. News [p. 82]
        A news Web site contains _____

        _____

    3. Informational [p. 82]
        An informational Web site contains _____

        _____

    4. Business/marketing [p. 82]
        A business/marketing Web site contains _____

        _____

    5. Educational [p. 82]
        An educational Web site contains _____

        _____

    6. Entertainment [p. 84]
        An entertainment Web site contains _____

        _____

7. Advocacy [p. 84]

An advocacy Web site contains _____

_____

8. Blog [p. 84]

A blog, or Web log, is _____

_____

A blogger is _____

_____

9. Wiki [p. 84]

A wiki is _____

_____

10. Content aggregator [p. 84]

A content aggregator is _____

_____

RSS 2.0 (Really Simple Syndication) is _____

_____

11. Personal [p. 84]

A personal Web site is _____

_____

F. Evaluating a Web site [p. 84]

The seven criteria for evaluating the value of a Web site are: affiliation, audience, authority, content, currency, design, and objectivity.

G. Multimedia on the Web [p. 85]

Multimedia refers to _____

_____

1. Graphics [p. 85]

A graphic, or graphical image, is _____

_____

Common file formats for graphical images on the Web:
- The JPEG format _____

  _____

- The GIF format _____

  _____

- The PNG format _____

  _____

A thumbnail is _____

2. Animation [p. 86]

Animation is _____

_____

An animated GIF uses _____

_____

3. Audio [p. 86]

Audio includes _____

_____

MP3 is _____

A player is _____

_____

Streaming is _____

_____

Streaming audio enables _____

_____

A podcast is_____

_____

4. Video [p. 88]

Video consists of _____

_____

The Moving Picture Experts Group (MPEG) defines a popular video
compression standard, the current one being called _____
Streaming video allows _____

_____

5. Virtual reality [p. 88]

Virtual reality (VR) is _____

_____

A VR world is _____

6. Plug-ins [p. 89]

A plug-in is _____

_____

V. Web publishing [p. 89]

Web publishing is _____

_____

VI. E-commerce [p. 91]

E-commerce (electronic commerce) is _____

M-commerce (mobile commerce) identifies _____

Types of e-commerce:

- Business-to-consumer (B2C) e-commerce consists of_____

  _____

  An electronic storefront contains _____

  _____

  A shopping cart allows _____
  An online auction is _____

  _____

- Consumer-to-consumer (C2C) e-commerce occurs _____

  _____

- Business-to-business (B2B) e-commerce occurs _____

  _____

VII. Other Internet services [p. 92]

In addition to the World Wide Web, many other Internet services are used widely.

A. E-mail [p. 92]

E-mail (electronic mail) is _____

_____

An e-mail program is used to _____

_____

An e-mail address is _____

_____

A user name is _____

_____

An address book contains _____
SMTP (simple mail transfer protocol) is _____

_____

POP3 is the latest version of POP (Post Office Protocol), which is_____

_____

B. FTP [p. 96]

FTP (File Transfer Protocol) is _____

_____

Uploading is _____

An FTP server is _____

_____

Anonymous FTP enables _____

_____

C. Newsgroups and message boards [p. 96]

A newsgroup is _____

_____

Usenet is _____

A news server is _____

A newsreader is _____

_____

Articles are _____

_____

To post an article means _____

_____

A thread (or threaded discussion) consists of_____

_____

When you subscribe to a newsgroup, its location is _____

_____

In a moderated newsgroup, the moderator reviews _____

_____

A message board is _____

_____

D. Mailing lists [p. 97]

A mailing list is _____

_____

When you subscribe to a mailing list, you add your name and e-mail address
to it; when you unsubscribe, you remove your name.

Some mailing lists are called LISTSERVs, _____

E. Chat rooms [p. 98]

A chat is _____

_____

Real time means _____

A chat room is _____

_____

A chat client is _____

_____

F. Instant messaging [p. 98]

Instant messaging (IM) is _____

_____

To use IM, you may have to install instant messenger software.

G. Internet telephony [p. 99]

Internet telephony (Voice over IP) is _____

_____

VIII. Netiquette [p. 100]

Netiquette is _____

_____

Some rules of netiquette:

Golden Rule: Treat _____

1. In e-mail, newsgroups, and chat rooms:

   *   Keep messages brief.
   *   Be careful when using _____
   *   Be polite.
   *   Read the message before you send it.
   *   Use meaningful_____
   *   Avoid sending or posting flames, which are _____

       _____

   *   Avoid sending spam, which is _____

       _____

   *   Do not use all capital letters, which is the equivalent of SHOUTING!
   *   Use emoticons to express _____

       _____

       _____

   *   Use abbreviations and acronyms for common phrases:

       _____

       _____

   *   Clearly identify a spoiler, which is _____

       _____

2. Read the FAQ (frequently asked questions), if one exists.

3. Do not assume _____

4. Never read _____

Self Test

Matching

1. _____ Web browser
2. _____ search engine
3. _____ player
4. _____ plug-in
5. _____ e-mail program
6. _____ FTP server
7. _____ newsreader
8. _____ chat client
9. _____ instant messaging
10. _____ netiquette

a. a computer that allows users to upload and download files using FTP

b. application software used to access and view Web pages

c. a software program, included with most browsers, used to participate in a newsgroup

d. a software program that extends the capability of a browser

e. a software program used to store multiple Web pages at a single site

f. the code of acceptable behaviors users follow on the Internet

g. a software program used to create, send, receive, forward, store, print, and delete messages

h. a software program that stores personal data on a client computer

i. a software program that can play the audio in MP3 files on your computer

j. a real-time communications service that notifies you when people are online and then allows you to exchange messages, for example

k. a software program used to find Web sites, Web pages, and Internet files

l. a software program through which you connect to a chat server to start a chat session

True/False

_____ 1. Although each network on the Internet is owned by a public or private organization, no single organization owns or controls the Internet.

_____ 2. Due to their smaller market share, national ISPs usually offer fewer services and generally have a smaller technical support staff than regional ISPs.

_____ 3. In general, the first portion of each IP address identifies the specific computer, and the last portion identifies the network.

_____ 4. To remind you visually that you have visited a location or document, some browsers change the color of a text link after you click it.

_____ 5. Newspapers and television and radio stations are some of the media that maintain news Web pages.

_____ 6. Two of the more common formats for graphical images on the Web are MP3 and MPEG.

_____ 7. When you send an e-mail message, an outgoing mail server that is operated by your Internet access provider determines how to route the message through the Internet and then sends the message.

_____ 8. Before you use a compressed file, you must decompress it with a compression program.

_____ 9. Some mailing lists are called LISTSERVs, named after a popular list software product.

_____ 10. To place an Internet telephone call, you need a dial-up Internet connection; Internet telephone service; a microphone or telephone; and Internet telephone software or a telephone adapter.

Multiple Choice

_____ 1. What group oversees research and sets standards and guidelines for many areas of the Internet?
   a. Advanced Research Projects Agency (ARPA)
   b. Uniform Resource Locator (URL)
   c. Joint Photographic Experts Group (JPEG)
   d. World Wide Web Consortium (W3C)

_____ 2. In the URL http://www.yahoo.com/travel/index.html, what is http://?
   a. protocol
   b. domain name
   c. path
   d. document name

_____ 3. For what type of images does the GIF format work best?
   a. scanned photographs
   b. line drawings and simple cartoons
   c. multi-hued artwork
   d. images with smooth color variations

_____ 4. What is a small version of a large graphical image you usually can click to display the full-sized image?
   a. tag
   b. marquee
   c. thumbnail
   d. player

_____ 5. What is a VR world?
   a. entire 3-D Web site that contains infinite space and depth
   b. Web site that joins a group of people with similar interests
   c. location on an Internet server that permits users to talk
   d. Web site where you bid on an item being sold by someone else

_____ 6. When you visit an online business through an electronic storefront, in what type of e-commerce are you participating?
   a. business-to-consumer (B2C) e-commerce
   b. consumer-to-consumer (C2C) e-commerce
   c. business-to-business (B2B) e-commerce
   d. consumer-to-business (C2B) e-commerce

_____ 7. What communications technology is used to retrieve e-mail from a server?
   a. SMTP (simple mail transfer protocol)
   b. POP (Post Office Protocol)
   c. http (Hypertext Transfer Protocol)
   d. ISP (Internet service protocol)

_____ 8. What is a previously entered newsgroup message called?
   a. spider
   b. crawler
   c. spoiler
   d. article

_____ 9. What enables users to speak to other users over the Internet using their computer?
   a. Web page wizards
   b. Web browsers
   c. instant messenger service
   d. voice over IP

_____ 10. Which of the following is *not* a rule of netiquette?
   a. keep messages brief, using proper grammar and spelling
   b. read the FAQ (frequently asked questions), if one exists
   c. assume all material is accurate and up to date
   d. be careful when using sarcasm and humor

Fill in the Blanks

1. Until 1995, NSFnet handled the bulk of the communications activity, or _____, on the Internet.

2. _____ is a not-for-profit Internet-related research and development project designed to improve on the inefficiencies of the Internet.

3. _____ access takes place when the modem in your computer uses a standard telephone line to connect to the Internet.

4. A(n) _____ server is an Internet server that usually is associated with an Internet access provider.

5. A Web _____ is a collection of related Web pages and associated items, such as documents and pictures, stored on a Web server.

6. A(n) _____ directory classifies Web pages into an organized set of categories, such as sports or shopping, and related subcategories.

7. A(n) _____ is a type of Web site that offers a variety of Internet services from a single, convenient location.

8. A(n) _____ is a digital representation of nontext information such as a drawing, chart, or photograph.

9. _____ is the process of transferring data in a continuous and even flow.

10. Many FTP sites allow _____, whereby anyone can transfer some, if not all, available files.

Complete the Table
TOP-LEVEL DOMAIN (TLD) ABBREVIATIONS

TLD Abbreviations	Type of Domain
_____	Commercial organizations, businesses, and companies
edu	_____
_____	Government agencies
mil	_____
_____	Network providers
org	_____
_____	Businesses of all sizes
pro	_____

Things to Think About

1. How is an ISP similar to, and different from, an OSP? Which would you use to access the Internet? Why?

2. Compared to conventional commerce, what are the advantages, and disadvantages, of e-commerce? For what products is e-commerce most, and least, suited? Why?

3. Why is a moderated newsgroup considered more valuable than a newsgroup that is not moderated? What topics might be dealt with more effectively in a newsgroup that is not moderated? Why?

4. What netiquette rules or guidelines do you think are most important? What rules are least important? Why?

Puzzle

Write the word described by each clue in the puzzle below. Words can be written forward or backward, across, up and down, or diagonally. The initial letter of each word already appears in the puzzle.

M								A	B	
				U				D		N
	M		D					N		
					L					
C	A							C		
			B							
S	U						T			
		P								
P	I						N			
	E		M	G		H	I			
S						O	M			

Appearance of motion created by displaying a series of still images

Music, speech, or any other sound

Communications lines that carry the heaviest traffic on the Internet

Software program that allows you to access and view Web pages

Computer that can access the contents of the storage area on a server

System on the Internet that stores domain names and their IP addresses

Provides high-speed connections over regular copper telephone lines

Digital representation of information such as a drawing or photograph

Starting page for a browser, similar to a book cover

Regional or national provider of access to the Internet

Type of numerical address that uniquely identifies each Internet computer

Built-in connection to another related Web page or part of a Web page

Special software that displays Web pages on handheld computers

Reviews the contents of a newsgroup article and posts it, if appropriate

Defines a popular video compression standard

Refers to any application that combines text with graphics, animation, audio, video, and/or virtual reality

Code of acceptable behaviors users should follow while on the Internet

Online area in which users conduct written discussions about a subject

Program used to participate in a newsgroup

Supplies Internet access along with many members-only features

Allows an e-commerce customer to collect purchases

Program that reads pages on Web sites in order to create a catalog of hits

Consists of an original newsgroup article and all subsequent replies

Copy a file from your computer to a Web site

Unique Web page address that tells a browser where to locate the page

A real-time typed conversation on a computer

To move content to your computer at regular intervals; Web servers can do this

A communications technology used by some outgoing mail servers

Business transaction that occurs over an electronic network

Self Test Answers

Matching	True/False	Multiple Choice	Fill in the Blanks
1. *b* [p. 75]	1. *T* [p. 70]	1. *d* [p. 70]	1. *traffic* [p. 70]
2. *k* [p. 78]	2. *F* [p. 72]	2. *a* [p. 77]	2. *Internet2* [p. 70]
3. *i* [p. 87]	3. *F* [p. 74]	3. *b* [p. 85]	3. *Dial-up* [p. 71]
4. *d* [p. 89]	4. *T* [p. 77]	4. *c* [p. 86]	4. *DNS* [p. 74]
5. *g* [p. 93]	5. *T* [p. 82]	5. *a* [p. 88]	5. *site* [p. 75]
6. *a* [p. 96]	6. *F* [p. 85]	6. *a* [p. 92]	6. *subject* [p. 78]
7. *c* [p. 96]	7. *T* [p. 94]	7. *b* [p. 95]	7. *portal* [p. 82]
8. *l* [p. 98]	8. *F* [p. 96]	8. *d* [p. 96]	8. *graphic* or *graphical image* [p. 85]
9. *j* [p. 98]	9. *T* [p. 97]	9. *d* [p. 99]	9. *Streaming* [p. 86]
10. *f* [p. 100]	10. *F* [p. 99]	10. *c* [p. 100]	10. *anonymous FTP* [p. 96]

Complete the Table

TOP-LEVEL DOMAIN (TLD) ABBREVIATIONS

TLD Abbreviations	Type of Domain
com	Commercial organizations, businesses, and companies
edu	*Educational institutions*
gov	Government agencies
mil	*Military organizations*
net	Network providers
org	*Nonprofit organizations*
biz	Businesses of all sizes
pro	*Certified professionals such as doctors, lawyers, and accountants*

Things to Think About

Answers will vary.

Puzzle Answer

M	S	P	E	N	O	B	K	C	A	B	T
T	I	N	U	I	U	D	N	N	D	R	N
A	M	C	D	O	A	R	I	S	A	N	E
H	E	U	R	O	R	M	L	C	E	C	T
C	A	G	L	O	A	G	G	W	R	C	I
H	I	P	A	T	B	N	S	E	H	L	Q
S	U	H	I	P	I	R	M	W	T	I	U
U	P	O	P	P	E	M	O	G	E	E	E
P	N	I	P	A	O	M	E	W	P	N	T
T		O	D	C	R	P	O	D	S	T	T
M	H	E	E	M	G	S	H	I	E	E	
S	R	O	T	A	R	E	D	O	M	A	R

DISCOVERING COMPUTERS 2007
STUDY GUIDE

CHAPTER 3
Application Software

Chapter Overview

This chapter illustrates how to start and use application software. It then presents an overview of a variety of business software, graphic and multimedia software, home/personal/educational software, and communications software. The chapter describes widely used utility programs and identifies various Web applications. Finally, learning aids and support tools for application software are presented.

Chapter Objectives

After completing this chapter, you should be able to:

- Identify the categories of application software
- Explain ways software is distributed
- Explain how to work with application software
- Identify the key features of widely used business programs
- Identify the key features of widely used graphics and multimedia programs

- Identify the key features of widely used home, personal, and educational programs
- Identify the types of application software used in communications
- Describe the function of several utility programs
- Discuss the advantages of using application software on the Web
- Describe the learning aids available for application software

Chapter Outline

I. Application software [p. 134]

Application software consists of _____

_____

- Packaged software is _____
- Custom software is _____
- Open source software is _____
- Shareware is _____
- Freeware is _____
- Public-domain software is _____

Product activation is _____

A. The role of system software [p. 135]

System software serves as _____

_____

Loading the operating system means _____

_____

B. Working with application software [p. 136]

The desktop is _____

_____

An icon is _____

_____

A button is _____

_____

To click a button requires _____

_____

The pointer is _____

A menu contains _____

A command is _____

_____

A submenu is _____

You can start an application by clicking its name on a menu or submenu.

Once started, an application displays in a window on the desktop.

A window is _____

_____

A title bar is _____

A file is _____

_____

A file name is _____

A dialog box is _____

_____

II. Business software [p. 138]

Business software is _____

_____

A. Word processing software [p. 138]

Word processing software, or a word processor, allows _____

_____

Word processing software features:

- Clip art is _____
- Margins are _____
- Wordwrap allows _____
- Scrolling is _____
- Search allows _____

  Replace allows _____
- A spelling checker reviews _____

  _____
- A header is _____

  A footer is _____

B. Developing a document [p. 141]

Many applications, such as word processing, allow you to create, edit, format,

print, and save documents.

When you create a document, you _____

_____

To edit a document means _____

_____

A clipboard is _____

_____

Pasting is _____

_____

Formatting involves _____

_____

A font is _____

- A serif font has _____
- A sans serif font is missing _____

Font size specifies _____

A point is _____

Font style adds _____

Saving is _____

_____

Printing is _____

_____

C. Spreadsheet software [p. 142]

Spreadsheet software allows _____

_____

A worksheet is _____

1. Spreadsheet organization [p. 143]

A spreadsheet file contains up to 255 related worksheets. On a worksheet, data is organized vertically in columns and horizontally in rows. A letter identifies each column, and a number identifies each row.

A cell is _____

Cells are identified by the column and row in which they are located (e.g., the cell at column B and row 10 is referred to as cell _____).

A label identifies _____

2. Calculations [p. 143]

A value is _____

_____

A formula performs _____

_____

A function is _____

_____

3. Recalculation [p. 144]

A powerful spreadsheet feature is that when data changes, the rest of the data in a worksheet is recalculated automatically.

What-if analysis is _____

_____

4. Charting [p. 144]

Charting shows the relationship of data in graphical form.

• Line charts show _____

_____

• Column charts (bar charts) display _____

_____

• Pie charts show _____

_____

D. Database software [p. 145]

A database is _____

Database software allows _____

_____

Most PC databases consist of tables organized in rows and columns.

- A record is _____

_____

- A field is _____

_____

- A query is _____

_____

E. Presentation graphics software [p. 146]

Presentation graphics software allows _____

_____

A slide show is _____

_____

Slide sorter view presents _____

_____

To import graphics means _____

_____

F. Note taking software [p. 147]

Note taking software is _____

_____

G. Personal information managers [p. 148]

A personal information manager (PIM) is _____

_____

H. PDA business software [p. 148]

The software on memory cards allows PDA users to _____

_____

I. Software suite [p. 148]

A software suite is _____

_____

Software suites offer two major advantages: _____

_____

J. Project management software [p. 149]

Project management software allows _____

_____

K. Accounting software [p. 149]

Accounting software helps _____

_____

L. Document management software [p. 150]

Document management software provides _____

_____

PDF is _____

_____

M. Enterprise computing software [p. 150]

Each functional unit of a large organization has specialized software
requirements, as outlined here:

- _____   - _____
- _____   - _____
- _____   - _____
- _____   - _____
- _____

III. Graphics and multimedia software [p. 151]

Power users often use sophisticated software to work with graphics and
multimedia.

A. Computer-aided design [p. 151]

Computer-aided design (CAD) software is _____

_____

B. Desktop publishing software (for the professional) [p. 152]

Desktop publishing (DTP) software enables _____

_____

DTP software is designed to support page layout, which is _____

_____

A color library is _____

C. Paint/image editing software (for the professional) [p. 152]

Paint software (illustration software) allows _____

_____

Image editing software provides _____

_____

    D. Photo editing software (for the professional) [p. 152]

       Professional photo editing software allows _____

       _____

    E. Video and audio editing software (for the professional) [p. 153]

       Video editing software allows _____

       _____

       Audio editing software lets users _____

       _____

       Filters are _____

    F. Multimedia authoring software [p. 154]

       Multimedia authoring software allows _____

       _____

    G. Web page authoring software [p. 154]

       Web page authoring software helps _____

       _____

IV. Software for home, personal, and educational use [p. 155]

    Most of the programs in this category are inexpensive, costing less than $100.

    A. Software suite (for personal use) [p. 156]

       A software suite (for personal use) combines _____

       _____

    B. Personal finance software [p. 156]

       Personal finance software is _____

       _____

       Online banking offers _____

       _____

    C. Legal software [p. 157]

       Legal software assists _____

       _____

    D. Tax preparation software [p. 157]

       Tax preparation software is used _____

       _____

    E. Desktop publishing software (for personal use) [p. 158]

       Personal DTP software can _____

       _____

F. Paint/image editing software (for personal use) [p. 158]

Personal paint/image editing software provides _____

_____

G. Photo editing software [p. 159]

Personal photo editing software allows _____

_____

H. Clip art/image gallery [p. 159]

A clip art/image gallery is _____

I. Video and audio editing software (for personal use) [p. 159]

With these programs, home users can _____

_____

J. Home design/landscaping software [p. 160]

Home design/landscaping software assists _____

_____

K. Reference and educational software [p. 160]

Reference software provides _____

_____

Educational software is_____

_____

Computer-based training (CBT) is _____

_____

L. Entertainment software [p. 160]

Entertainment software includes _____

_____

V. Application software for communications [p. 161]

Users have a variety of software options relative to communications:

E-mail (electronic mail) is _____

_____

FTP allows _____

_____

A Web browser allows _____

_____

Video conferencing/telephone calls permit _____

_____

A newsgroup/message board is _____

_____

A chat room permits _____

_____

Instant messaging is _____

_____

Blogging is _____

_____

Blog software, or blogware, allows a blogger to _____

_____

VI. Popular utility programs [p. 162]
   A virus is _____

_____

Widely used utility programs include:

- Antivirus programs protect _____

  _____

- A personal firewall detects and protects _____

  _____

- Spyware removers detect _____

  _____

- Anti-spam programs remove _____
- Web filters restrict _____
- Pop-up blockers stop_____
- File managers provide _____

  _____

- File compression utilities shrink _____

  _____

- Backup utilities allow users to _____

  _____

- CD/DVD burners write _____

  _____

- Personal computer maintenance utilities fix_____

  _____

VII. Application software on the Web [p. 163]

A Web application is _____

_____

A. Application service providers [p. 164]

An application service provider (ASP) is _____

_____

The five categories of ASPs are:

- _____

- _____

- _____

- _____

- _____

VIII. Learning aids and support tools for application software [p. 164]

Learning aids provided by applications include:

Online Help is _____

_____

- Web-based help provides _____

_____

- A wizard is _____

_____

- A template is _____

_____

A. Web-based training [p. 166]

Web-based training (WBT) is _____

_____

Distance learning (DL) is _____

_____

Self Test

Matching

1. _____ computer-aided design (CAD) software

2. _____ desktop publishing (DTP) software

3. _____ paint software

4. _____ image editing software

5. _____ multimedia authoring software

6. _____ personal finance software

7. _____ legal software

8. _____ home design/landscaping software

9. _____ educational software

10. _____ entertainment software

a. used to prepare legal documents and provide legal information to individuals

b. used to combine text, graphics, audio, video, and animation into an interactive presentation

c. includes interactive games and videos

d. used in creating engineering, architectural, and scientific designs

e. used to balance a checkbook, pay bills, track income and expenses, and track investments

f. used to add special effects like shadows or glows to images

g. used to draw pictures, shapes, and other graphical images with various on-screen tools

h. used to edit digital photographs by removing red-eye or adding special effects

i. used to create Web pages, in addition to organizing and maintaining Web sites

j. used to create sophisticated documents containing text, graphics, and many colors

k. used to assist with the design or remodeling of a house, deck, or landscape

l. used to teach a particular skill, like typing

True/False

_____ 1. A button is a small image displayed on the screen that represents a program, a document, or some other object.

_____ 2. A header is text that appears at the bottom of each page.

_____ 3. Formatting is important because the overall look of a document can affect its ability to communicate effectively.

_____ 4. Only a small fraction of the columns and rows in a spreadsheet are displayed on the computer screen at one time.

_____ 5. In a database, a field contains information about a given person, product, or event, while a record contains a specific piece of information within a field.

_____ 6. Presentation graphics software provides an array of predefined presentation formats that define complementary colors and other items on the slides.

_____ 7. Most PIMs do not include an appointment calendar, address book, or notepad.

_____ 8. The applications within a software suite are likely to use different interfaces and to have entirely unique features.

_____ 9. A Web filter restricts access to specified Web sites.

_____ 10. To access a Web application, you simply visit the Web site that offers the program.

Multiple Choice

_____ 1. What is loaded, or copied, into memory from the computer's hard disk each time you start your computer?
a. operating system
b. software application
c. software package
d. utility program

_____ 2. What is a title bar?
a. a small image that displays on the screen to represent a program
b. an on-screen work area that uses common graphical elements
c. a horizontal space at the top of a window that contains the window's name
d. an instruction that causes a computer program to perform a specific action

_____ 3. What happens when you format a document?
a. text, numbers, or graphical images are inserted using an input device
b. changes are made to the document's existing content
c. the appearance of the document is changed
d. the document is copied from memory to a storage medium

_____ 4. How many rows and columns does a spreadsheet typically have?
a. 256 columns and 256 rows
b. 65,536 columns and 65,536 rows
c. 65,536 columns and 256 rows
d. 256 columns and 65,536 rows

_____ 5. Which of the following shows a trend during a period of time, as indicated by a rising or falling line?
a. bar chart
b. line chart
c. column chart
d. pie chart

_____ 6. In a personal information manager (PIM), for what purpose is a notepad used?
a. to record ideas, reminders, and other important information
b. to schedule activities for a particular day and time
c. to enter and maintain names, addresses, and telephone numbers
d. to design and produce sophisticated documents

_____ 7. What type of software might a general contractor use to manage a home-remodeling schedule or a publisher use to coordinate the process of producing a textbook?
   a. home design/landscaping software
   b. project management software
   c. desktop publishing software
   d. presentation graphics software

_____ 8. What type of software can be used to modify sound clips and usually includes filters designed to enhance sound quality?
   a. audio editing software
   b. video editing software
   c. image editing software
   d. photo editing software

_____ 9. What type of software products often use a computer-based training (CBT) approach?
   a. educational software
   b. home design/landscaping software
   c. reference software
   d. clip art/image gallery software

_____ 10. What automated assistant does word processing software use to help you create memorandums, meeting agendas, fax cover sheets, and letters?
   a. online help
   b. FAQs
   c. tutorials
   d. wizards

Fill in the Blanks

1. _____ software is mass produced, copyrighted retail software that meets the needs of a wide variety of users, not just a single user or company.

2. _____ software is provided for use, modification, and redistribution, without copyright restrictions.

3. A(n) _____ contains a series of commands from which you make selections.

4. A single _____ is about 1/72 of an inch in height.

5. A(n) _____ performs calculations on the data in the worksheet and displays the resulting value in a cell.

6. A software _____ is a collection of individual programs sold as a single package.

7. Web page _____ software helps users of all skill levels create Web pages that include graphical images, video, audio, animation, and other special effects.

8. _____ banking offers access to account balances and provides bill paying services.

9. A(n) _____ program attempts to remove spam before it reaches your e-mail inbox.

10. _____ is the delivery of education at one location while the learning takes place at other locations.

Complete the Table

POPULAR SOFTWARE PROGRAMS FOR HOME/PERSONAL/EDUCATIONAL USE

Application Software	Popular Programs
_____	• Microsoft Works • Sun OpenOffice.org
_____	• Intuit Quicken • Microsoft Money
_____	• H&R Block Kiplinger's WILLPower • Nolo Quicken Legal Business
_____	• Broderbund PrintMaster • Microsoft Publisher
_____	• Adobe Photoshop Elements • Microsoft Digital Image
_____	• H&R Block TaxCut • Intuit TurboTax
_____	• Broderbund ClickArt • Nova Development Art Explosion
_____	• Broderbund 3D Home Architect • ValuSoft LandDesigner
_____	• Microsoft Encarta • Rand McNally TripMaker

Things to Think About

1. What word processing features would be most useful to an author composing a short story? To a publicist creating a newsletter? To a student writing a term paper? Why?

2. Why is a spreadsheet's capability to perform what-if analysis important to business executives?

3. What types of software would be particularly useful to business travelers? Why?

4. What types of communications software would be most used by a teenager? A college student? A business professional? Why?

Puzzle

Use the given clues to complete the crossword puzzle.

Across

1. Potentially damaging computer program that affects a computer by altering the way it works without the user's knowledge or permission
5. Small image that represents a program, document, or other object
6. Reviews the spelling of words in a document
9. Collection of data organized to allow access, retrieval, and use of the data
11. Type of program that protects a computer against viruses
13. Type of education in which students learn by using computer exercises
16. Software that helps organize personal information
17. Text that appears at the bottom of each page in a document
19. Utility that shrinks the size of a file
21. Third-party organization that distributes software and services on the Web
23. Type of training that uses Internet technology and consists of application software on the Web
25. Type of Internet filter/blocker that stops advertisements from displaying on Web pages
27. A rectangular area of the screen that displays a program, data, and/or information
28. Intersection of a spreadsheet column and row
29. Software used to produce sophisticated documents with text and graphics

Down

2. Type of software that serves as the interface between the user, the application software, and the computer's hardware
3. An automated assistant that helps a user complete a task by asking questions and then performing actions based on the responses
4. Name assigned to a specific design of characters
7. Utility that detects and protects a personal computer from unauthorized intrusions
8. A predefined formula that performs common calculations such as adding the values in a group of cells
10. Any sound stored and produced by a computer
12. Enables users to enter handwritten comments and then save the page as part of a notebook
14. Writes text, graphics, audio, and video files on a recordable or rewritable CD or DVD
15. Collection of individual software applications sold as a single package
18. A collection of drawings, diagrams, maps, and photographs that you can insert into documents
20. PIM capability used to record ideas, reminders, and other information
22. On-screen work area that can display graphical elements
24. Transmission of messages via a computer network
26. About 1/72 of an inch in height

Self Test Answers

Matching	True/False	Multiple Choice	Fill in the Blanks
1. *d* [p. 151]	1. *F* [p. 136]	1. *a* [p. 135]	1. *Packaged* [p. 134]
2. *j* [p. 152]	2. *F* [p. 140]	2. *c* [p. 137]	2. *Open source* [p. 135]
3. *g* [p. 152]	3. *T* [p. 141]	3. *c* [p. 141]	3. *menu* [p. 137]
4. *f* [p. 152]	4. *T* [p. 143]	4. *d* [p. 143]	4. *point* [p. 141]
5. *b* [p. 154]	5. *F* [p. 145]	5. *b* [p. 144]	5. *formula* [p. 143]
6. *e* [p. 156]	6. *T* [p. 146]	6. *a* [p. 148]	6. *suite* [p. 148]
7. *a* [p. 157]	7. *F* [p. 148]	7. *b* [p. 149]	7. *authoring* [p. 154]
8. *k* [p. 160]	8. *F* [p. 148]	8. *a* [p. 153]	8. *Online* [p. 156]
9. *l* [p. 160]	9. *T* [p. 162]	9. *a* [p. 160]	9. *anti-spam* [p. 162]
10. *c* [p. 160]	10. *T* [p. 163]	10. *d* [p. 165]	10. *DL* or *Distance learning* [p. 166]

Complete the Table

POPULAR SOFTWARE PROGRAMS FOR HOME/PERSONAL/EDUCATIONAL USE

Application Software	Popular Programs
Software Suite (for personal use)	• Microsoft Works • Sun OpenOffice.org
Personal Finance	• Intuit Quicken • Microsoft Money
Legal	• H&R Block Kiplinger's WILLPower • Nolo Quicken Legal Business
Desktop Publishing (for Personal Use)	• Broderbund PrintMaster • Microsoft Publisher
Photo Editing (for Personal Use)	• Adobe Photoshop Elements • Microsoft Digital Image
Tax Preparation	• H&R Block TaxCut • Intuit TurboTax
Clip Art/Image Gallery	• Broderbund ClickArt • Nova Development Art Explosion
Home Design/Landscaping	• Broderbund 3D Home Architect • ValuSoft LandDesigner

Application Software	Popular Programs
Reference	• Microsoft Encarta • Rand McNally TripMaker

Things to Think About

Answers will vary.

Puzzle Answer

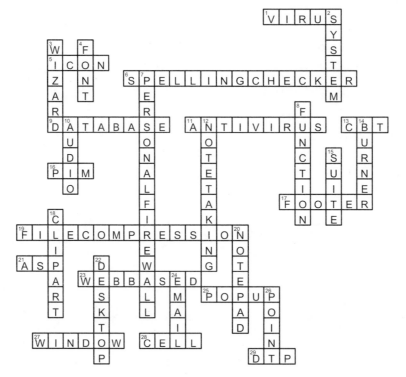

DISCOVERING COMPUTERS 2007
STUDY GUIDE

CHAPTER 4

The Components of the System Unit

Chapter Overview

This chapter presents the components of the system unit; describes how memory stores data, instructions, and information; and discusses the sequence of operations that occur when a computer executes an instruction. The chapter includes a comparison of various personal computer processors on the market today. The chapter also discusses how to clean a system unit.

Chapter Objectives

After completing this chapter, you should be able to:

- Differentiate among various styles of system units
- Identify chips, adapter cards, and other components of a motherboard
- Describe the components of a processor and how they complete a machine cycle
- Identify characteristics of various personal computer processors on the market today
- Define a bit and describe how a series of bits represents data
- Explain how programs transfer in and out of memory

- Differentiate among the various types of memory
- Describe the types of expansion slots and adapter cards
- Explain the difference among a serial port, a parallel port, a USB port, a FireWire port, and other ports
- Describe how buses contribute to a computer's processing speed
- Identify components in mobile computers and mobile devices
- Understand how to clean a system unit

Chapter Outline

I. The system unit [p. 184]

The system unit is _____

_____

The chassis is _____

A. The motherboard [p. 186]

The motherboard, or system board, is _____

_____

A chip is _____

_____

An integrated circuit contains _____

_____

A transistor acts _____

II. Processor [p. 187]

The processor (also called a central processing unit or CPU) interprets _____

_____

Some computer and chip manufacturers use the term microprocessor to refer to

_____

Most devices connected to a computer communicate with the processor to carry
out a task. Processors contain the control unit and the arithmetic logic unit (ALU).

A. The control unit [p. 187]

The control unit directs _____

_____

B. The arithmetic logic unit [p. 188]

The arithmetic logic unit (ALU) performs _____

_____

- Arithmetic operations include_____

_____

- Comparison operations involve _____

_____

C. Machine cycle [p. 188]

For every instruction, the processor repeats a set of four basic operations
comprising a machine cycle:

- Fetching is_____
- Decoding is _____
- Executing is _____
- Storing is_____

Pipelining is _____

_____

D. Registers [p. 189]

Registers are _____

_____

E. The system clock [p. 189]

The system clock controls _____

_____

Each tick of the system clock is a clock cycle. Many of today's processors are

superscalar and can _____

Clock speed is _____

_____

A hertz is _____

Current PC processors have clock speeds in the gigahertz range.

- Gigahertz (GHz) equals _____

Some computer professionals measure a computer's speed in MIPS (millions

of instructions per second).

F. Comparison of personal computer processors [p. 190]

Intel is a leading manufacturer of personal computer processors. Intel makes

the Pentium, Pentium M, Celeron, Xeon, and Itanium processors.

Intel-compatible processors have _____

_____

An IBM (or Motorola) processor has _____

_____

Hyper-Threading (HT) Technology improves _____

_____

A dual-core processor is _____

_____

A multicore processor is _____

_____

Intel's Centrino mobile technology integrates _____

_____

A system on a chip processor integrates _____

_____

G. Buying a personal computer [p. 192]

Buying a new computer requires a decision about the platform (i.e., IBM-

compatible versus Apple), the processor speed, and whether or not you might

be able to upgrade the processor on your existing computer.

Viiv technology is designed to _____

_____

H. Heat sinks, heat pipes, and liquid cooling [p. 193]
   A heat sink is _____

   _____

   A heat pipe cools _____

   _____

   Liquid cooling technology uses _____

   _____

I. Parallel processing [p 194]
   Parallel processing speeds processing time by using _____

   _____

III. Data representation [p. 194]
   Human speech is analog because _____

   _____

   Most computers are digital because they recognize _____

   _____

   Computers use the binary system, which has only two digits to represent the
   electronic states of off (0) and on (1).
   A bit is_____
   A byte is _____
   Patterns called coding schemes are used to represent data:
   • ASCII is _____
   • EBCDIC is _____
   • Unicode is _____

IV. Memory [p. 197]
   Memory consists of_____

   _____

   Memory stores three basic categories of items:
   (1) _____
   (2) _____
   (3) _____
   The stored program concept is _____

   _____

A. Bytes and addressable memory [p. 197]

An address is _____

_____

B. Memory sizes [p. 197]

Manufacturers state memory and storage sizes in terms of the number of bytes the chip or device has available for storage.

- A kilobyte (KB or K) is _____
- A megabyte (MB) is _____
- A gigabyte (GB) is _____
- A terabyte (TB) is _____

C. Types of memory [p. 197]

Memory can be volatile or nonvolatile.

Volatile memory loses _____

_____

Nonvolatile memory does _____

_____

D. RAM [p. 198]

RAM (random access memory), also called main memory, consists of _____

_____

Most RAM is volatile, so items needed in the future must be saved.

Basic types of RAM:

- Dynamic RAM (DRAM) chips must be _____

_____

Variations of DRAM chips:

Synchronous DRAM (SDRAM) chips are _____

_____

Double Data Rate SDRAM (DDR SDRAM) chips are_____

_____

Rambus DRAM (RDRAM) chips are _____

_____

- Static RAM (SRAM) chips are _____

_____

- Magnetoresistive RAM (MRAM) stores _____

_____

A memory module is _____

_____

Memory slots hold _____

_____

Three types of memory modules are SIMMs, DIMMs, and RIMMs.
- A SIMM (single inline memory module) has _____

_____

- A DIMM (dual inline memory module) has _____

_____

- A RIMM (Rambus inline memory module) has_____

_____

1. RAM configurations [p. 199]
   The amount of RAM a computer requires depends _____

   _____

E. Cache [p. 201]
   Cache is used to _____

   _____

   Memory cache stores _____

   _____

   Layers of memory cache:
   - L1 cache is _____
   - L2 cache is _____
     Advanced transfer cache (ATC) is _____
   - L3 cache is _____

F. ROM [p. 201]
   Read-only memory (ROM) refers to_____

   _____

   - Firmware contains _____

   _____

   - A PROM (programmable read-only memory) chip is _____

   _____

   Microcode is _____

   _____

   - An EEPROM (electrically erasable programmable read-only memory)
     chip allows _____

   _____

G. Flash memory [p. 202]

Flash memory is _____

_____

H. CMOS [p. 203]

Complementary metal-oxide semiconductor (CMOS) memory stores _____

_____

I. Memory access times [p. 203]

Access time is _____

_____

Memory access times are measured in nanoseconds (ns), which are _____

_____

V. Expansion slots and adapter cards [p. 204]

An expansion slot is _____

_____

An adapter card (expansion card) is _____

_____

A peripheral is_____

_____

A sound card enhances _____

A video card, or graphics card, converts _____

With Plug and Play, the computer can _____

_____

A. PC Cards, flash memory cards, and USB flash drives [p. 205]

Notebook and other mobile computers have at least one PC Card slot, which is

_____

A PC Card (originally called PCMCIA card) is _____

_____

The Personal Computer Memory Card International Association developed __

_____

Flash memory cards allow _____

_____

A USB flash drive is _____

_____

Hot plugging allows _____

_____

VI. Ports and connectors [p. 206]

A port is _____

The term *jack* sometimes is used _____

_____

A connector joins _____

- Male connectors have _____

- Female connectors have _____

A gender changer is _____

_____

A. Serial ports [p. 207]

A serial port is _____

_____

Serial ports (e.g., the COM port) connect _____

_____

B. Parallel ports [p. 208]

A parallel port is _____

_____

C. USB ports [p. 208]

A USB (universal serial bus) port can _____

_____

USB 2.0 is _____

_____

Daisy chain means _____

_____

A USB hub plugs _____

_____

D. FireWire ports [p. 209]

A FireWire port (previously an IEEE 1394 port) connects _____

_____

A FireWire hub is _____

_____

E. Special-purpose ports [p. 209]

Four special-purpose ports are MIDI, SCSI, IrDA, and Bluetooth.

1. MIDI port [p. 209]

A MIDI (Musical Instrument Digital Interface) port connects _____

A synthesizer creates _____

2. SCSI port [p. 210]

    A SCSI (small computer system interface) port is _____

    _____

3. IrDA port [p. 210]

    An IrDA (Infrared Data Association) port transmits _____

    _____

    A fast infrared port is _____

    _____

4. Bluetooth port [p. 210]

    Bluetooth technology uses _____

    _____

VII. Buses [p. 211]

      A bus is an electrical channel that allows _____

      _____

      Buses consist of two parts: a data bus and an address bus.

      - A data bus transfers _____

      - An address bus transfers _____

      The bus width, or size of the bus, determines_____

      _____

      Word size is _____

      Basic types of buses:

      - A system bus is _____

      - An expansion bus allows _____

      A. Expansion bus [p. 212]

          The types of expansion buses on the motherboard determine the types of
          expansion cards you can add.

          Types of expansion buses:

          - The PCI (Peripheral Component Interconnect) bus is_____

            _____

          - The Accelerated Graphics Port (AGP) is _____

            _____

          - The USB (universal serial bus) and FireWire bus eliminate _____

            _____

      •   The PC Card bus is _____

VIII. Bays [p. 212]

A bay is _____

Drive bays typically hold _____

      •   An external drive bay allows _____

          _____

      •   An internal drive bay is _____

          _____

IX. Power supply [p. 213]

The power supply is _____

An AC adapter is _____

X. Mobile computers and devices [p. 213]

Like their desktop counterparts, mobile computers and devices have a motherboard that contains electronic components that process data. The difference between the two types of computers is _____

_____

XI. Putting it all together [p. 215]

Many components of the system unit influence the speed and power of a computer. These include: _____

_____

XII. Keeping your computer clean [p. 216]

Preventive maintenance on your computer requires a few basic products:

      • _____   • _____

      • _____   • _____

      • _____   • _____

Self Test

Matching

1. _____ PC Card slot

2. _____ PCMCIA card

3. _____ flash memory card

4. _____ USB port

5. _____ MIDI port

6. _____ SCSI port

7. _____ IrDA port

8. _____ Bluetooth port

9. _____ PCI bus

10. _____ FireWire bus

a. bus that speeds processing by storing frequently used instructions and data

b. uses radio waves to transmit data between two devices

c. port used by wireless devices to transmit signals to a computer via light waves

d. port that can connect up to 127 different peripherals with a single connector

e. notebook and mobile computers have at least one

f. original name of PC Cards

g. port designed to absorb and ventilate heat produced by electrical components

h. special high-speed parallel port used to attach disk drives and printers

i. removable memory device that allows users to transfer data and information conveniently from mobile devices to their PCs

j. bus that eliminates the need to install expansion cards into expansion slots

k. special type of serial port designed to connect the system unit to a musical instrument

l. used with video cards and high-speed network cards

True/False

_____ 1. On a personal computer, the electronic components and most storage devices reside outside the system unit.

_____ 2. Taken together, fetching, decoding, executing, and storing comprise a machine cycle.

_____ 3. A brand of Intel processor called the Xeon is designed for less expensive PCs.

_____ 4. The American Standard Code for Information Interchange (ASCII) is used primarily on mainframe computers.

_____ 5. When the computer is powered on, certain operating system files load from a storage device and remain in RAM as long as the computer is running.

_____ 6. With a single inline memory module (SIMM), the pins on opposite sides of the circuit board do not connect and thus form two sets of contacts.

_____ 7. Accessing data in memory can be more than 200,000 times slower than accessing data on a hard disk.

_____ 8. A peripheral is a device that connects to the system unit and is controlled by the processor in the computer.

_____ 9. Unlike other cards, a flash memory card can be changed without having to open the system unit or restart the computer.

_____ 10. A standard wall outlet's direct current ranging from 5 to 12 volts is unsuitable for use with a computer, which requires AC power ranging from 115 to 120 volts.

Multiple Choice

_____ 1. On a personal computer, what normally is located *outside* the system unit?
   a.   keyboard and monitor
   b.   processor and memory module
   c.   ports and connectors
   d.   all of the above

_____ 2. In the machine cycle, what is the process of decoding?
   a.   obtaining an instruction or data item from memory
   b.   translating an instruction into a command a computer can execute
   c.   carrying out the commands
   d.   writing a result to memory

_____ 3. Most high-performance PCs use a version of which kind of processor?
   a.   the Celeron microprocessor
   b.   the Motorola microprocessor
   c.   the Pentium microprocessor
   d.   the Alpha microprocessor

_____ 4. A group of eight bits, called a byte, provides enough different combinations of 0s and 1s to represent how many individual characters?
   a.   8
   b.   32
   c.   256
   d.   1,024

_____ 5. Which of the following is an example of volatile memory?
   a.   RAM
   b.   ROM
   c.   CMOS
   d.   flash memory

_____ 6. Generally, home users running Windows XP and using standard application software, such as word processing, should have at least how much RAM?
    a. 8 MB
    b. 16 MB
    c. 32 MB
    d. 256 MB

_____ 7. When a processor needs an instruction or data, in what order does it search memory?
    a. first RAM, then L1 cache, then L2 cache, then L3 cache (if it exists)
    b. first L3 cache (if it exists), then L1 cache, then RAM, then L2 cache
    c. first L2 cache, then L3 cache (if it exists), then RAM, then L1 cache
    d. first L1 cache, then L2 cache, then L3 cache (if it exists), then RAM

_____ 8. Instead of port, which term sometimes is used to identify audio and video ports?
    a. connector
    b. bus
    c. jack
    d. receiver

_____ 9. Originally developed as an alternative to the slower speed serial ports, parallel ports often are used to connect what to the system unit?
    a. mouse
    b. keyboard
    c. modem
    d. printer

_____ 10. Like the clock speed at which a processor executes, the clock speed for a bus is measured in what unit?
    a. milliseconds (ms)
    b. megahertz (MHz)
    c. nanoseconds (ns)
    d. kilobytes (KB)

Fill in the Blanks

1. A(n) _____ processor is a chip with two or more separate processors.

2. As the cost of _____ declines, experts predict it could replace both DRAM and SRAM.

3. _____ cache helps speed the processes of the computer because it stores frequently used instructions and data.

4. Current processors include _____, a type of L2 cache built directly on the processor chip.

5. ROM chips called _____ contain permanently written data, instructions, or information.

6. _____ memory is a type of nonvolatile memory that can be erased electronically and reprogrammed, similarly to EEPROM.

7. Many of today's computers support _____, which means the computer automatically can configure peripherals as you install them.

8. A(n) _____ plugs into a USB port on the system unit and contains multiple USB ports into which cables from USB devices are plugged.

9. A(n) _____ port allows you to connect up to 63 devices together.

10. A(n) _____ is an opening inside the system unit in which you can install additional equipment.

Complete the Table

MEMORY AND STORAGE SIZES

Term	Abbreviation	Approximate Number of Bytes	Approximate Number of Pages of Text
_____	KB or K	1 thousand bytes	_____
Megabyte	_____	_____	500
_____	GB	_____	500,000
_____	_____	1 trillion bytes	500,000,000

Things to Think About

1. If you were to purchase a personal computer today, what type of processor would it have? Why?

2. Why do people upgrade their processors instead of buying a new computer? What form of processor upgrade seems easiest? Why?

3. How do coding schemes make it possible for humans to interact with computers? Why do people usually not realize that coding scheme conversions are occurring?

4. How is the system unit for a notebook computer similar to, and different from, the system unit for a desktop computer? Why do you think a notebook computer usually is more expensive than a desktop computer with the same capabilities?

Puzzle

Write the word described by each clue in the puzzle below. Words can be written forward or backward, across, up and down, or diagonally. The initial letter of each word already appears in the puzzle.

	S		S				U		M	C
				G	F					C
		H						A		
M							G	W		
P			A					R		
	B			M		C	P			
			P		A					
		B				R				
M				K						
		I		B	A					
	D		U							
S										

Box-like case that houses the electronic components of a computer

Main circuit board in the system unit

CPU component that directs and coordinates most computer operations

Unit in which some computer professionals measure a CPU's speed

CPU component that performs arithmetic and comparison operations

One system clock cycle per second

Opening in the motherboard into which a processor chip is inserted

Smallest unit of data a computer can represent

The most widely used coding system to represent data

Coding scheme capable of representing all the world's current languages

Temporary storage place for data, instructions, and information

Abbreviation for approximately 1,000 bytes

Abbreviation for approximately one million bytes

Abbreviation for approximately one billion bytes

Memory chips that can be read from and written to

Small circuit board on which RAM chips usually reside

Improves processing time in most of today's computers

Memory chips storing data that only can be read

Technology that provides high speeds and consumes little power

Thin, credit card-sized device that adds capabilities to a mobile computer

Interface, or point of attachment, of an external device to the system unit

Type of interface that connects devices by transmitting data one bit at a time

Type of interface that connects devices by transferring more than one bit at a time

Type of port that connects a musical instrument to the system unit

Type of high-speed, specialized parallel port

Type of port necessary for wireless devices to transmit signals to a computer

Channel that allows devices inside and attached to the system unit to communicate

Number of bits a processor can interpret and execute at a given time

Besides FireWire, another type of bus that eliminates the need to install cards into expansion slots

Open spaces that most often hold disk drives

Another name for a video card

Adapter used by external peripherals

Abbreviation for approximately 1 billion bytes

Bus designed by Intel to improve the speed with which 3-D graphics and video transmit

Previously called an IEEE 1394 port

Self Test Answers

Matching	True/False	Multiple Choice	Fill in the Blanks
1. *e* [p. 205]	1. *F* [p. 184]	1. *a* [p. 184]	1. *multicore* [p. 190]
2. *f* [p. 205]	2. *T* [p. 188]	2. *b* [p. 188]	2. *magnetoresistive RAM* or *MRAM* [p. 199]
3. *i* [p. 205]	3. *F* [p. 190]	3. *c* [p. 190]	
4. *d* [p. 208]	4. *F* [p. 195]	4. *c* [p. 195]	3. *Memory* [p. 201]
5. *k* [p. 209]	5. *T* [p. 198]	5. *a* [p. 197]	4. *advanced transfer cache* [p. 201]
6. *h* [p. 210]	6. *F* [p. 199]	6. *d* [p. 200]	5. *firmware* [p. 202]
7. *c* [p. 210]	7. *F* [p. 203]	7. *d* [p. 201]	6. *Flash* [p. 202]
8. *b* [p. 210]	8. *T* [p. 204]	8. *c* [p. 206]	7. *Plug and Play* [p. 205]
9. *l* [p. 212]	9. *T* [p. 205]	9. *d* [p. 208]	8. *USB hub* [p. 208]
10. *j* [p. 212]	10. *F* [p. 213]	10. *b* [p. 212]	9. *FireWire* [p. 209]
			10. *bay* [p. 212]

Complete the Table

MEMORY AND STORAGE SIZES

Term	Abbreviation	Approximate Number of Bytes	Approximate Number of Pages of Text
Kilobyte	KB or K	1 thousand bytes	*1/2*
Megabyte	*MB*	*1 million bytes*	500
Gigabyte	GB	*1 billion bytes*	500,000
Terabyte	*TB*	1 trillion bytes	500,000,000

Things to Think About

Answers will vary.

Puzzle Answer

I	S	C	S	I			U	S	O	M	C
D			E	B	G	F	S	L	O	E	C
I	S	H	R		P	I	B	T	A	M	O
M	Y	E	I	G		R	H	G	W	O	N
P	A	R	A	L	L	E	L	P	O	R	T
S	B	T	L	M	R	W	C	P	R	Y	R
P	E	Z	P	B	A	I	A	C	D	M	O
I	V	B	O	D	S	R	C	C	S	O	L
M	I	A	R	K	C	E	H	A	I	D	U
T	R	I	T	B	I	A	E	R	Z	U	N
D	D		U	N	I	C	O	D	E	L	I
S	Y	S	T	E	M	U	N	I	T	E	T

DISCOVERING COMPUTERS 2007
STUDY GUIDE

CHAPTER 5
Input

Chapter Overview

Input is any data or instructions you enter into the memory of a computer. This chapter describes the various techniques of input and several commonly used input devices. Topics presented include the keyboard, mouse, and other pointing devices; voice input; input devices for PDAs, smart phones, and Tablet PCs; digital cameras; video input; scanners and reading devices; terminals; biometric input; and input devices for physically challenged users.

Chapter Objectives

After completing this chapter, you should be able to:

- Define input
- List the characteristics of a keyboard
- Describe different mouse types and how they work
- Summarize how various pointing devices work
- Explain how voice recognition works
- Describe various input devices for PDAs, smart phones, and Tablet PCs
- Explain how a digital camera works
- Describe the uses of PC video cameras, Web cams, and video conferencing
- Discuss various scanners and reading devices and how they work
- Explain the types of terminals
- Summarize the various biometric devices
- Identify alternative input devices for physically challenged users

Chapter Outline

I. What is input? [p. 234]

Input is _____

_____

- Data is _____

_____

- A program is _____

_____

A command is _____

_____

User response is _____

_____

II.   What are input devices? [p. 236]
      An input device is _____

      _____

III. The keyboard [p. 236]
      A keyboard is _____

      _____

      An enhanced keyboard has _____

      _____

      Function keys are _____

      _____

      A toggle key is _____

      _____

      The insertion point, also known as the cursor in some applications, is _____

      _____

      A gaming keyboard is _____

      _____

      A. Keyboard connections [p. 238]
          A wireless (or cordless) keyboard is _____

          _____

      B. Keyboard ergonomics [p. 238]
          An ergonomic keyboard has _____

          _____

          The goal of ergonomics is_____

          _____

IV.   Pointing devices [p. 239]
      A pointing device is _____

      _____

      A pointer is _____

      _____

V. Mouse [p. 239]

A mouse is _____

_____

A mouse pointer is _____

_____

A. Mouse types [p. 239]

- A mechanical mouse has _____

_____

A mouse pad is _____

_____

- An optical mouse uses _____

_____

- A wireless (or cordless) mouse is _____

_____

B. Using a mouse [p. 240]

In addition to pointing, you can perform several operations using the mouse, including: _____

_____

_____

Mouse gestures minimize _____

_____

VI. Other pointing devices [p. 241]

Although the mouse is the most widely used pointing device, some users work with other pointing devices.

A. Trackball [p. 241]

A trackball is _____

_____

B. Touchpad [p. 241]

A touchpad is _____

_____

C. Pointing stick [p. 242]

A pointing stick is _____

_____

D. Joystick and wheel [p. 242]

A joystick is _____

A wheel is _____
_____

E. Audio player control pad [p. 242]
    The control pad on an audio player is _____
    _____

    The iPod's Click Wheel is used to _____
    _____

F. Gamepad [p. 242]
    A gamepad is _____
    _____

G. Light pen [p. 242]
    A light pen is _____
    _____

H. Touch screen [p. 243]
    A touch screen is _____
    _____

I. Pen input [p. 243]
    With pen input, users _____
    _____

    A stylus is _____
    _____

    A digital pen is _____
    _____

    Many handheld computers use handwriting recognition software that
    translates _____
    _____

    A graphics tablet is _____
    _____

    A cursor is_____
    _____

    A digitizer is _____
    _____

VII. Voice input [p. 245]
      Voice input is _____

Voice recognition, or speech recognition, is _____

_____

- With speaker-dependent software, the computer makes _____

_____

- Speaker-independent software has _____

_____

- Discrete speech requires _____

_____

- Continuous speech is _____

_____

A. Audio input [p. 246]

   Audio input is _____

_____

   MIDI (musical instrument digital interface) is _____

_____

VIII. Input for PDAs, smart phones, and Tablet PCs [p. 247]

   A. PDAs [p. 247]

      Data can be input into a PDA in a variety of ways, including:

_____

_____

      A portable keyboard is _____

   B. Smart phones [p. 248]

      1. Text messaging [p. 248]

         Text messaging is used to _____

_____

_____

      2. Instant messaging [p. 248]

         Instant messaging (IM) is _____

_____

_____

      3. Picture messaging [p. 249]

         With picture messaging, users can _____

_____

_____

C. Tablet PCs [p. 249]

A docking station is _____

_____

IX. Digital cameras [p. 250]

A digital camera allows _____

_____

To work with images from a digital camera, you download (transfer a copy of) the images to a personal computer.

Basic types of digital cameras:

• A studio camera is _____

_____

• A field camera is _____

_____

• A point-and-shoot camera is _____

_____

A. Digital camera quality [p. 252]

Resolution describes _____

_____

The higher the resolution, the better the image quality.

Some manufacturers use dots per inch to represent a digital camera's resolution.

A pixel is _____

_____

Digital camera resolutions range from _____

Pixels per inch (ppi) is _____

_____

• Optical resolution is _____

_____

• Enhanced resolution uses _____

_____

X. Video input [p. 253]

Video input is _____

_____

To input video, the analog video signal must be converted into a digital signal.

A video capture card is _____

A digital video (DV) camera is _____

A. PC video cameras [p. 253]
   A PC video camera, or PC camera, is _____

   During a video telephone call, both parties can _____

B. Web cams [p. 254]
   A Web cam is _____

   A streaming cam shows _____

C. Video conferencing [p. 254]
   A video conference is _____

   A whiteboard is _____

XI. Scanners and reading devices [p. 255]
   A source document is _____

   Scanners and reading devices make the input process more efficient by capturing
   data directly from source documents.
   A. Optical scanner [p. 255]
      An optical scanner, or scanner, is _____

      A flatbed scanner creates _____

      Like a digital camera, the quality of a scanner is measured by its resolution.
      OCR (optical character recognition) software can _____

      Image processing consists of _____

      An image processing system is _____

B. Optical readers [p. 257]

An optical reader is _____

_____

   1. Optical character recognition [p. 257]

     Optical character recognition (OCR) is _____

     _____

     _____

     Most OCR devices include _____

     _____

     OCR characters often are used on turnaround documents. A turnaround
     document is _____

     _____

   2. Optical mark recognition [p. 257]

     Optical mark recognition (OMR) is _____

     _____

     _____

C. Bar code reader [p. 258]

A bar code reader, also called a bar code scanner, uses _____

_____

A bar code is _____

_____

The UPC (Universal Product Code) bar code is used by _____

_____

_____

D. RFID readers [p. 259]

RFID (radio frequency identification) is _____

_____

An RFID reader reads _____

_____

E. Magnetic stripe card readers [p. 260]

A magnetic stripe card reader (magstripe reader) is _____

_____

F. MICR reader [p. 260]

MICR (magnetic-ink character recognition) is_____

_____

An MICR reader converts_____

The banking industry almost exclusively uses MICR for check processing.

G. Data collection devices [p. 261]

A data collection device obtains data _____

_____

XII. Terminals [p. 261]

A terminal consists of _____

_____

A dumb terminal has _____

_____

A smart terminal has _____

_____

A. Point-of-sale terminals [p. 261]

A point of sale (POS) is _____

_____

A POS terminal is used to _____

_____

B. Automated teller machines [p. 262]

An automated teller machine (ATM) is _____

_____

A personal identification number (PIN) verifies _____

_____

XIII. Biometric input [p. 262]

Biometrics is _____

_____

A biometric identifier is _____

_____

A biometric device translates _____

_____

A fingerprint scanner captures _____

_____

A face recognition system captures _____

_____

A hand geometry system measures _____

_____

A voice verification system compares _____

_____

A signature verification system recognizes _____

_____

An iris recognition system is _____

_____

Retinal scanners scan _____

_____

A smart card stores _____

_____

XIV. Putting it all together [p. 265]

Many factors influence the type of input devices you may use, including _____

_____

_____

_____

XV. Input devices for physically challenged users [p. 266]

The Americans with Disabilities Act (ADA) requires _____

_____

_____

A keyguard is _____

_____

An on-screen keyboard displays _____

_____

A head-mounted pointer is _____

_____

With gesture recognition, the computer will _____

_____

Self Test

Matching

1. _____ command
2. _____ enhanced keyboard
3. _____ cordless keyboard
4. _____ mouse
5. _____ trackball
6. _____ touchpad
7. _____ pointing stick
8. _____ light pen
9. _____ stylus
10. _____ portable keyboard

a. handheld input device that can detect the presence of light

b. light-sensing input device that reads printed text and graphics and then transmits the results

c. keyboard with 12 function keys along the top, 2 CTRL keys, 2 ALT keys, and a set of arrow keys

d. provides multiple users with an area on which they can write or draw

e. small metal or plastic device that uses pressure instead of ink to write on a mobile device

f. pressure-sensitive pointing device shaped like a pencil eraser, positioned between keys

g. full-sized keyboard that can be attached to and removed from a PDA

h. instruction that causes a program to perform a specific action

i. small, flat, rectangular pointing device that is sensitive to pressure and motion

j. widely used pointing device designed to fit comfortably under the palm of your hand

k. stationary pointing device with a ball on its top that is rotated with the thumb or fingers

l. battery-powered device that transmits data using wireless technology

True/False

_____ 1. Desktop computer keyboards typically have from 101 to 155 keys.

_____ 2. The command associated with a function key depends on the program you are using.

_____ 3. An optical mouse is less precise than a mechanical mouse, but it also is slightly less expensive.

_____ 4. A pointing stick does not need additional desk space and does not require cleaning like a mechanical mouse or trackball.

_____ 5. The best voice recognition programs are 50 to 60 percent accurate, which means the software may interpret as many as 4 in 10 words incorrectly.

_____ 6. PDA is the electronic music industry's standard that defines how digital music devices represent sounds electronically.

_____ 7. The smaller the number of pixels a digital camera uses to capture an image, the better the quality of the image.

_____ 8. To transfer recorded images to a hard disk, users connect DV cameras directly to a USB port or a FireWire port on the system unit.

_____ 9. To participate in a video conference, you need video conferencing software, a microphone, speakers, and a video camera attached to your computer.

_____ 10. The banking industry almost exclusively uses MICR (magnetic-ink character recognition) for check processing.

Multiple Choice

_____ 1. Which of the following is a collection of unprocessed text, numbers, images, audio, and video?
   a. programs
   b. user responses
   c. commands
   d. data

_____ 2. Which kind of key is used to switch between two states each time a user presses the key?
   a. toggle key
   b. function key
   c. alternate key
   d. application key

_____ 3. In a graphical user interface, which of the following is a small symbol on the screen whose location and shape changes as a user moves a pointing device?
   a. cursor
   b. pointer
   c. icon
   d. opticon

_____ 4. What is the most widely used pointing device today?
   a. touchpad
   b. trackball
   c. joystick
   d. mouse

_____ 5. What pointing device is most often found on notebook computers?
   a. mouse
   b. touchpad
   c. joystick
   d. trackball

_____ 6. What input device often is used in kiosks located in stores, hotels, airports, and museums?
    a. joystick
    b. touch screen
    c. pointing stick
    d. touchpad

_____ 7. A 2304 x 1728 ppi digital camera has how many pixels?
    a. 2,304 pixels down the vertical edge and 1,728 pixels across the horizontal edge
    b. 2,304 pixels per vertical inch and 1,728 pixels per horizontal inch
    c. 2,304 pixels across the horizontal edge and 1,728 pixels down the vertical edge
    d. 2,304 pixels per horizontal inch and 1,728 pixels per vertical inch

_____ 8. What device captures data directly from source documents?
    a. optical scanners
    b. ergonomic keyboards
    c. pointing devices
    d. all of the above

_____ 9. What type of bar code is used by the United States Postal Service?
    a. POSTNET
    b. Codabar
    c. UPC — Universal Product Code
    d. Code 39

_____ 10. Which of the following stores the biometric data on its thin microprocessor?
    a. digital camera
    b. scanner
    c. smart card
    d. whiteboard

Fill in the Blanks

1. The _____ is a symbol that indicates where on the screen the next character you type will display.

2. The goal of _____ is to incorporate comfort, efficiency, and safety into the design of items in the workplace.

3. A(n) _____ is a rectangular rubber or foam pad that provides better traction for a mouse than the top of a desk.

4. Given text that has been entered using a stylus or digital pen, computers can use _____ software that translates the handwritten letters and symbols into characters that the computer can process.

5. Some graphics tablets use a(n) _____, which is a device that looks similar to a mouse, except that it has a window with crosshairs.

6. Most voice recognition software allows you to speak in a flowing conversational tone, called _____ speech.

7. Instead of calling someone's smart phone or cellular telephone, users can enter and send typed messages using _____ messaging.

8. With _____ messaging, users can send graphics, pictures, video clips, and sound files, as well as short text messages to another smart phone with a compatible service.

9. _____ allows you to convert paper documents such as reports, memos, and procedure manuals into an electronic form.

10. Computers with a capability called _____ have the potential to recognize sign language, read lips, track facial movements, or follow eye gazes.

Complete the Table
MOUSE OPERATIONS

Operation	Mouse Action
_____	Move the mouse across a flat surface until the pointer on the desktop is positioned on the item of choice.
_____	Press and release the primary mouse button, which usually is the left mouse button.
_____	Press and release the secondary mouse button, which usually is the right mouse button.
_____	Quickly press and release the left mouse button twice without moving the mouse.
_____	Quickly press and release the left mouse button three times without moving the mouse.
_____	Point to an item, hold down the left mouse button, move the item to the desired location on the screen, and then release the left mouse button.
_____	Point to an item, hold down the right mouse button, move the item to the desired location on the screen, and then release the right mouse button.
_____	Roll the wheel forward or backward.
_____	Press the wheel button while moving the mouse on the desktop.

Operation	Mouse Action
	Press the wheel toward the right or left.

Things to Think About

1. Two types of input are data and instructions (programs, commands, and user responses). What type of input device (keyboard, pointing devices, scanners, and so on) can be used to enter each type of input?

2. How is a notebook computer keyboard different from a desktop computer keyboard? What keys might be left off of, or serve more than one purpose on, a notebook keyboard?

3. What pointing device would you most like to have with a desktop computer? What pointing device would you most like to have with a notebook computer? Why?

4. How do scanners and reading devices make the input process more efficient and accurate? For what, if any, types of input are scanners and reading devices unsuitable? Why?

Puzzle

The terms described by the phrases below are written below each line in code. Break the code by writing the correct term above the coded word. Then, use your code to translate the final sentence.

1. Any data or instructions entered into the memory of a computer

   RMKFG

2. Collection of facts, figures, and symbols that is processed into information

   WZGZ

3. Commonly used input device containing keys that are pressed to enter data

   PVBYLZIW

4. Found on the right side of many desktop computer keyboards

   MFNVIRX PVBKZW

5. Symbol that indicates where on the screen the next character typed will appear

   RMHVIGRLM KLRMG

6. Four keys: one pointing up, one pointing down, one pointing left, and one pointing right

   ZIILD PVBH

7. Key that switches between two different states, often indicated by status lights

   GLTTOV PVB

8. Small symbol on the screen that usually takes the shape of a block arrow, I-beam, or pointing hand

   KLRMGVI

9. Input device often used with game software and flight and driving simulation software

   QLBHGRXP

10. Allows you to tap areas of the display with your finger to enter data

    GLFXS HXIVVM

11. Allows you to take and store photographed images digitally instead of on traditional film

    WRTRGZO XZNVIZ

12. Factor that describes the sharpness and clearness of an image

    IVHLOFGRLM

13. Meeting between geographically separated people who use a network or the Internet to transmit data

    ERWVL XLMUVIVMXV

14. Original form of data captured with scanners or reading devices

    HLFIXV WLXFNVMG

15. Light-sensing input device that reads printed material and translates it into a form the computer can use

    HXZMMVI

16. Type of document designed to be returned to the company that creates and sends it

    GFIMZILFMW

17. Identification consisting of a set of vertical lines
    and spaces of different widths

    YZI XLWV

GBKRHGH FHRMT GSV NLOGILM PVBYLZIW, DSRXS RH HKORG ZMW

XLMGLFIVW GL URG VZXS SZMW DRGS GSV NLHG XLNNLMOB FHVW PVBH

FMWVI GSV HGILMTVHG URMTVIH, XZM GBKV NLIV GSZM GSIVV GRNVH

UZHGVI GSZM GBKRHGH FHRMT Z GIZWRGRLMZO PVBYLZIW.

Self Test Answers

Matching	True/False	Multiple Choice	Fill in the Blanks
1. *h* [p. 235]	1. *F* [p. 236]	1. *d* [p. 234]	1. *insertion point* or *cursor* [p. 237]
2. *c* [p. 236]	2. *T* [p. 236]	2. *a* [p. 237]	2. *ergonomics* [p. 238]
3. *l* [p. 238]	3. *F* [p. 239]	3. *b* [p. 237]	3. *mouse pad* [p. 239]
4. *j* [p. 239]	4. *T* [p. 242]	4. *d* [p. 239]	4. *handwriting recognition* [p. 243]
5. *k* [p. 241]	5. *F* [p. 246]	5. *b* [p. 241]	5. *cursor* [p. 244]
6. *i* [p. 241]	6. *F* [p. 246]	6. *b* [p. 243]	6. *continuous* [p. 246]
7. *f* [p. 242]	7. *F* [p. 252]	7. *b* [p. 252]	7. *text* [p. 248]
8. *a* [p. 242]	8. *T* [p. 253]	8. *a* [p. 255]	8. *picture* [p. 249]
9. *e* [p. 243]	9. *T* [p. 254]	9. *a* [p. 258]	9. *Image processing* [p. 256]
10. *g* [p. 248]	10. *T* [p. 260]	10. *c* [p. 264]	10. *gesture recognition* [p. 266]

Complete the Table

MOUSE OPERATIONS

Operation	Mouse Action
Point	Move the mouse across a flat surface until the pointer on the desktop is positioned on the item of choice.
Click	Press and release the primary mouse button, which usually is the left mouse button.
Right-click	Press and release the secondary mouse button, which usually is the right mouse button.
Double-click	Quickly press and release the left mouse button twice without moving the mouse.
Triple-click	Quickly press and release the left mouse button three times without moving the mouse.
Drag	Point to an item, hold down the left mouse button, move the item to the desired location on the screen, and then release the left mouse button.

Operation	Mouse Action
Right-drag	Point to an item, hold down the right mouse button, move the item to the desired location on the screen, and then release the right mouse button.
Rotate wheel	Roll the wheel forward or backward.
Press wheel button	Press the wheel button while moving the mouse on the desktop.
Tilt wheel	Press the wheel toward the right or left.

Things to Think About

Answers will vary.

Puzzle Answer

1. Any data or instructions entered into the memory of a computer

   input
   RMKFG

2. Collection of facts, figures, and symbols that is processed into information

   data
   WZGZ

3. Commonly used input device containing keys that are pressed to enter data

   keyboard
   PVBYLZIW

4. Found on the right side of many desktop computer keyboards

   numeric keypad
   MFNVIRX PVBKZW

5. Symbol that indicates where on the screen the next character typed will appear

   insertion point
   RMHVIGRLM KLRMG

6. Four keys: one pointing up, one pointing down, one pointing left, and one pointing right

   arrow keys
   ZIILD PVBH

7. Key that switches between two different states, often indicated by status lights

   toggle key
   GLTTOV PVB

8. Small symbol on the screen that usually takes the shape of a block arrow, I-beam, or pointing hand

   pointer
   KLRMGVI

9. Input device often used with game software and flight and driving simulation software

   joystick
   QLBHGRXP

10. Allows you to tap areas of the display with your finger to enter data

    touch screen
    GLFXS HXIVVM

11. Allows you to take and store photographed images digitally instead of on traditional film

    digital camera
    WRTRGZO XZNVIZ

12. Factor that describes the sharpness and clearness of an image

    resolution
    IVHLOFGRLM

13. Meeting between geographically separated people who use a network or the Internet to transmit data

    video conference
    ERWVL XLMUVIVMXV

14. Original form of data captured with scanners or reading devices

    source document
    HLFIXV WLXFNVMG

15. Light-sensing input device that reads printed material and translates it into a form the computer can use

    scanner
    HXZMMVI

16. Type of document designed to be returned to the company that creates and sends it

    turnaround
    GFIMZILFMW

17. Identification consisting of a set of vertical lines and spaces of different widths

    bar code
    YZI XLWV

Typists using the Maltron keyboard, which is split and
GBKRHGH FHRMT GSV NZOGILM PVBYLZIW, DSRXS RH HKORG ZMW

contoured to fit each hand with the most commonly used keys
XLMGLFIVW GL URG VZXS SZMW DRGS GSV NLHG XLNNLMOB FHVW PVBH

under the strongest fingers, can type more than three times
FMWVI GSV HGILMTVHG URMTVIH, XZM GBKV NLIV GSZM GSIVV GRNVH

faster than typists using a traditional keyboard.
UZHGVI GSZM GBKRHGH FHRMT Z GIZWRGRLMZO PVBYLZIW.

DISCOVERING COMPUTERS 2007

STUDY GUIDE

CHAPTER 6

Output

Chapter Overview

Computers process and organize data (input) into information (output). This chapter describes the various methods of output and several commonly used output devices. Output devices presented include flat-panel displays; CRT monitors; printers; speakers, headphones, and earphones; fax machines and fax modems; multifunction peripherals; data projectors; and force-feedback joysticks, wheels, and gamepads.

Chapter Objectives

After completing this chapter, you should be able to:

- Describe the four categories of output
- Summarize the characteristics of LCD monitors, LCD screens, and plasma monitors
- Describe the characteristics of a CRT monitor and factors that affect its quality
- Explain the relationship between graphics chips and monitors
- Describe various ways to print
- Differentiate between a nonimpact printer and an impact printer

- Summarize the characteristics of ink-jet printers, photo printers, laser printers, thermal printers, mobile printers, label and postage printers, and plotters and large-format printers
- Describe the uses of speakers, headphones, and earphones
- Identify the output characteristics of fax machines and fax modems, multifunction peripherals, data projectors, joysticks, wheels, and gamepads
- Identify output options for physically challenged users

Chapter Outline

I. What is output? [p. 300]

Output is _____

_____

Four basic categories of output:

- Text consists of _____

  _____

- Graphics are _____

  _____

- Audio is _____

  _____

- Video consists of _____

  _____

An output device is _____

_____

II. Display devices [p. 302]

A display device, or display, is _____

_____

The information displayed, or soft copy, exists _____

_____

A display device consists of a screen, or projection surface, and the components
that produce the information on the screen.

A monitor is _____

Most display devices are color, but some are monochrome.

- Monochrome means _____

III. Flat-panel displays [p. 302]

A flat-panel display is _____

_____

A. LCD monitors and screens [p. 302]

An LCD monitor, also called a flat panel monitor, uses _____

_____

A monitor's footprint is _____

_____

B. LCD technology [p. 304]

A liquid crystal display (LCD) uses _____

_____

- An active-matrix, or TFT (thin-film transistor), display uses _____

_____

- Organic LED (OLED) uses _____

  _____

- A passive-matrix display uses _____

  _____

C. LCD quality [p. 304]

Resolution is _____

A pixel is _____

Native resolution is _____

Response time is _____

_____

A nit is _____

_____

The candela is _____

_____

Pixel pitch (or dot pitch) is _____

_____

Contrast ratio describes _____

_____

D. Graphics chips, ports, and LCD monitors [p. 305]

The graphics processing unit controls _____

_____

A DVI (Digital Video Interface) port enables _____

_____

An S-video port allows _____

_____

Current video standards include:

- _____   • _____

- _____   • _____

The bit depth (color depth) is _____

E. Plasma monitors [p. 306]

A plasma monitor is _____

_____

F. Televisions [p. 306]

Digital television (DTV) offers _____

_____

HDTV (high-definition television) is _____

_____

IV. CRT monitors [p. 307]

A CRT monitor is _____

_____

A cathode-ray tube (CRT) is _____

_____

The dots of phosphor material that coat a CRT screen combine to form pixels.
A monitor's viewable size is _____

_____

The ENERGY STAR program encourages _____

_____

Electromagnetic radiation (EMR) is _____

_____

MPR II is _____

A. Quality of a CRT monitor [p. 308]

Refresh (or scan) rate is _____

_____

B. Graphics chips and CRT monitors [p. 308]

The greater the video card's bit depth _____

_____

V. Printers [p. 310]

A printer is _____

_____

Printed information, also called hard copy or printout, exists _____

_____

- Portrait orientation is _____
- Landscape orientation is _____

A. Producing printed output [p. 311]

Bluetooth printing works by _____

_____

Infrared printing works by _____

_____

B. Nonimpact printers [p. 312]

A nonimpact printer forms _____

Commonly used nonimpact printers are ink-jet printers, photo printers, laser printers, thermal printers, mobile printers, label and postage printers, plotters, and large-format printers.

C. Ink-jet printers [p. 312]

An ink-jet printer is _____

_____

Dots per inch (dpi) is _____

_____

D. Photo printers [p. 314]

A photo printer is _____

_____

E. Laser printers [p. 315]

A laser printer is _____

_____

Laser printers use software to interpret a page description language (PDL).

A page description language (PDL) tells _____

Common PDLs:

• PCL (Printer Control Language) is _____

• PostScript is _____

Toner is _____

_____

F. Thermal printers [p. 317]

A thermal printer generates _____

_____

Special types of thermal printers:

• A thermal wax-transfer printer generates _____

_____

• A dye-sublimation printer (or digital photo printer) uses _____

_____

G. Mobile printers [p. 317]

A mobile printer is _____

_____

H. Label and postage printers [p. 318]

A label printer is _____

_____

A postage printer is _____

_____

Internet postage is _____

I.   Plotters and large-format printers [p. 318]

Plotters are _____

_____

A large-format printer creates _____

_____

J.   Impact printers [p. 318]

An impact printer forms _____

_____

Near letter quality (NLQ) output is _____

_____

1. Dot-matrix printers [p. 319]

A dot-matrix printer is _____

_____

Dot-matrix printers use continuous-form paper, which connects _____

_____

2. Line printers [p. 319]

A line printer is_____

_____

Popular types of line printers:

• A band printer prints_____

_____

• A shuttle-matrix printer moves_____

_____

VI. Speakers, headphones, and earphones [p. 320]

An audio output device is _____

_____

• Speakers are _____
   Satellite speakers are_____
   A subwoofer boosts _____

• With headphones or earphones, only the user can _____
   The difference between earphones (earbuds) or headphones is _____

_____

Voice output occurs _____

_____

Internet telephony allows _____

_____

VII. Other output devices [p. 322]
      Many output devices are available for specific uses and applications:
      A. Fax machines and fax modems [p. 322]
          A fax machine is _____

          _____

          A fax is _____

          _____

          A fax modem is_____

          _____

      B. Multifunction peripherals [p. 323]
          A multifunction peripheral (or all-in-one device) is_____

          _____

      C. Data projectors [p. 323]
          A data projector is _____

          _____

          • An LCD projector uses _____

             _____

          • A digital light processing (DLP) projector uses _____

             _____

      D. Force-feedback joysticks, wheels, and gamepads [p. 324]
          Force feedback is _____

          _____

VIII. Putting it all together [p. 325]
       Many factors influence the type of output devices you should use, including: ____

       _____

       _____

  IX. Output devices for physically challenged users [p. 326]
       Output devices available for users with disabilities include_____

       _____

       _____

       A Braille printer outputs _____

Self Test

Matching

1.	_____	ink-jet printer
2.	_____	photo printer
3.	_____	laser printer
4.	_____	thermal printer
5.	_____	label printer
6.	_____	plotter
7.	_____	large-format printer
8.	_____	dot-matrix printer
9.	_____	band printer
10.	_____	shuttle-matrix printer

a. used in specialized fields such as engineering and drafting

b. uses a row of charged wires to draw an electrostatic pattern on specially coated paper

c. generates images by pushing electrically heated pins against heat-sensitive paper

d. produces images when tiny wire pins on a print head mechanism strike an inked ribbon

e. high-speed, high-quality nonimpact printer operating in a manner similar to a copy machine

f. prints fully formed characters when hammers strike a horizontal, rotating band

g. used by graphic artists to create photo-realistic-quality color prints

h. uses one or more colored pens or a scribing device to draw on paper or transparencies

i. produces photo-lab-quality pictures as well as prints everyday documents

j. forms characters and graphics by spraying tiny drops of liquid ink

k. prints on an adhesive-type material that can be placed on a variety of items

l. moves a series of print hammers back and forth horizontally at incredibly high speeds

True/False

_____ 1. Lower contrast ratios represent colors better.

_____ 2. The number of colors that a video card can display is determined by its bit depth, or the number of bits it uses to store information about each pixel.

_____ 3. Today, all broadcast stations must transmit analog signals, as mandated by the FCC.

_____ 4. In the past, CRT monitor screens were flat, but current models have slightly curved screens to reduce eyestrain and fatigue.

_____ 5. Higher-resolution monitors use fewer pixels, providing a rougher image.

_____   6. With an ink-jet printer, a higher dpi means the drops of ink are larger, which provides a lower quality image.

_____   7. PostScript is used in fields such as desktop publishing and graphic art because it is designed for complex documents with intense graphics and colors.

_____   8. Some companies use near letter quality (NLQ) impact printers for routine jobs such as printing mailing labels, envelopes, and invoices.

_____   9. When headphones are in use, anyone within listening distance can hear the output.

_____   10. An advantage of a multifunction peripheral is that it is significantly less expensive than if you purchase a printer, scanner, copy machine, and fax machine separately.

Multiple Choice

_____   1. What do notebook computers and mobile devices often use?
   a. CRT monitors
   b. gas plasma monitors
   c. LCD monitors
   d. all of the above

_____   2. How is a monitor's viewable size measured?
   a. in square inches, stating the area of the screen
   b. vertically, from the top-left corner to the bottom-left corner
   c. horizontally, from the top-left corner to the top-right corner
   d. diagonally, from one corner of the casing to the other

_____   3. Which of the following is a program encouraging manufacturers to create devices that require little power when they are not in use?
   a. VESA
   b. ENERGY STAR
   c. HDTV
   d. EMR

_____   4. On what does the quality of a CRT monitor or display depend?
   a. resolution
   b. dot pitch
   c. refresh rate
   d. all of the above

_____   5. A device transmits output to a printer via radio waves in which type of printing?
   a. Bluetooth
   b. infrared
   c. large-format
   d. PDL

_____   6. What type of printer often can read media directly from a digital camera,
            without the aid of a computer?
            a. thermal printers
            b. photo printers
            c. portable printers
            d. postage printers

_____   7. What type of nonimpact printer typically costs more than ink-jet printers, but
            also is much faster?
            a. dot-matrix printers
            b. thermal printers
            c. line printers
            d. laser printers

_____   8. What tells a laser printer how to lay out the contents of a printed page?
            a. digital language processor (DLP)
            b. language character display (LCD)
            c. page description language (PDL)
            d. nonimpact language quantifier (NLQ)

_____   9. Which of the following is *not* a commonly used type of impact printer?
            a. ink-jet printer
            b. dot-matrix printer
            c. band printer
            d. shuttle-matrix printer

_____ 10. What type of data projector uses tiny mirrors to reflect light, producing crisp,
            bright, colorful images that remain in focus and can be seen clearly even in a
            well-lit room?
            a. LCD projector
            b. large-format projector
            c. digital light processing (DLP) projector
            d. electrostatic projector

Fill in the Blanks

1. _____ is the most advanced form of digital television, working
    with digital broadcast signals, transmitting digital sound, supporting wide screens,
    and providing resolutions up to 1920 x 1080 pixels.

2. With _____ such as Microsoft's Xbox 360 and Sony's
    PlayStation 3, the output device often is a television.

3. Refresh rate is the number of times per second the screen is redrawn and is
    expressed in _____ .

4. _____ is a set of standards that defines acceptable levels of EMR
    (electromagnetic radiation) for a monitor.

5. A high-quality CRT monitor will provide a vertical refresh rate of at least
    _____ Hz.

6. A hard copy can be printed in portrait or _____ orientation.

7. A laser printer creates images using _____ and a laser beam.

8. A(n) _____ printer is a small, lightweight, battery-powered printer that allows a mobile user to print from a notebook computer.

9. _____ is digital postage you buy and print right from your PC.

10. _____ are sophisticated printers used to produce high-quality drawings such as blueprints, maps, and circuit diagrams.

Complete the Table
SUGGESTED OUTPUT DEVICES BY USER

User	Monitor	Printer
Home	_____	Ink-jet color printer or photo printer
Small office/home office	19- or 21-inch LCD monitor Color LCD screen on Tablet PC, PDA, or smart phone	_____ _____ _____
Mobile	_____ _____	Mobile color printer; ink-jet color printer; laser printer for in-office use (black-and-white or color); photo printer
Power	23-inch LCD monitor	_____ _____ _____
Large business	_____ _____	High-speed laser printer; color laser printer; line printer; label printer

Things to Think About

1. Why is output printed on paper, which is a flexible material, called hard copy while output displayed on a screen, which is firm to the touch, is called soft copy?

2. Why are flat panel monitors more expensive than CRT monitors? What advantages do flat panel monitors offer? Will flat panel monitors ever completely replace CRT monitors? Why or why not?

3. Using Figure 6-12 on page 310, answer each question about your current printer requirements. Based on your answers, what type of printer would you buy? Why?

4. How important is audio to you? Would you consider adding higher-quality stereo speakers, a subwoofer, or headphones to your personal computer? Why or why not?

Puzzle

All of the words described below appear in the puzzle. Words may be either forward or backward, across, up and down, or diagonal. Circle each word as you find it.

```
Q T A Y S M L I R M E Y K I L J B K O A H D B
F O J P U N E U E O D E W Z E B H Q Z N W T W
Q N Y I P I B U S S I P W Q Z Z T L O F D P J
G E B X X L I Q O V Y A D F U Y S P R R Q I N
Z R Y E V Z R C L A M C J R D I M T S C X R L
B T Y L Z D E W U W Q S F L N P I P M Z H C D
I F F E M R T H T G Y D G M O A E T D T Y S O
A T M U U Q N S I H I N L P R T Q N P P F T T
V U B V A T I Y O V G A I T A N F E O S Z S P
W X X G I T R L N J L L R R Y Q D C V U H O I
K Y V Y Z D P H B N D O H R V T D U Y V S P T
U S R P M O E K A D P S A U I R F B U T P V C
D J I J G K V O I U E C Y B A L F D T L G K H
H E P P U W K Y C R T U R H S L V F B D M Z N
B B P D Z W S U F A K E W R A I K Z T P O C N
P X V E T N V E D P R L S T M Z L F F V N V R
Y O T R S J R O J F A D P X U T B C E T I T E
M U Q A O L A N V J M A P H G R N A G V T D G
M T W R I C P B G C N T R M N E D P G H O H R
C P Y F P D N I I E D P F A X H O O F M R C B
C U D N N L V M L Y Y T S O G G D P I R H T B
O T P I J P D H T O O T E U L B K W H R Z W Q
N D M R Z K I F R V Q W Z O E G O H M R T G B
```

Data that has been processed into a useful form

The number of bits a video card uses to store pixel information

The processor chip contained on a video card that performs calculations used to display images on the screen

Display device consisting of a screen housed in a plastic or metal case

Desktop monitor that uses a liquid crystal display; also called an LCD monitor

Another name for an active-matrix display

Type of port that accepts digital signals directly, eliminating the need for analog-to-digital conversion

The most advanced form of digital television

Single point in an electronic image

Printing that uses radio waves to transmit output

Sharpness or clarity of an image

Vertical distance between pixels on a monitor

Speed with which the monitor redraws images on the screen

Measure of refresh rate

Converts digital output into an analog signal

Standard supported today by just about every video card

Output device that produces text and graphics on a physical medium

Orientation taller than it is wide

Orientation wider than it is tall

Printing in which the device communicates using infrared light waves

Unit in which ink-jet printer resolution is measured

Tells a laser printer how to lay out a page

Page description language commonly used in desktop publishing

Powdered ink used by laser printers

Communications device that transmits computer-prepared documents over telephone lines

A magnetic field that travels at the speed of light

Projector that uses liquid crystal display technology and its own light source to display information shown on a computer screen

Projector that uses tiny mirrors to reflect light to produce images that can be seen clearly even in a well-lit room

A term for printed information

Self Test Answers

Matching	True/False	Multiple Choice	Fill in the Blanks
1. *j* [p. 312]	1. *F* [p. 304]	1. *c* [p. 303]	1. *HDTV (high-definition television)* [p. 306]
2. *i* [p. 314]	2. *T* [p. 306]	2. *d* [p. 307]	2. *game consoles* [p. 307]
3. *e* [p. 315]	3. *F* [p. 306]	3. *b* [p. 307]	3. *hertz or Hz* [p. 308]
4. *c* [p. 317]	4. *F* [p. 307]	4. *d* [p. 308]	4. *MPR II* [p. 308]
5. *k* [p. 318]	5. *F* [p. 308]	5. *a* [p. 311]	5. *68* [p. 308]
6. *a* [p. 318]	6. *F* [p. 313]	6. *b* [p. 314]	6. *landscape* [p. 310]
7. *g* [p. 318]	7. *T* [p. 316]	7. *d* [p. 315]	7. *toner* [p. 316]
8. *d* [p. 319]	8. *T* [p. 318]	8. *c* [p. 316]	8. *mobile* [p. 317]
9. *f* [p. 319]	9. *F* [p. 321]	9. *a* [p. 318]	9. *Internet postage* [p. 318]
10. *l* [p. 319]	10. *T* [p. 323]	10. *c* [p. 324]	10. *Plotters* [p. 318]

Complete the Table

SUGGESTED OUTPUT DEVICES BY USER

User	Monitor	Printer
Home	*17- or 19-inch LCD monitor*	Ink-jet color printer or photo printer
Small office/home office	19- or 21-inch LCD monitor Color LCD screen on Tablet PC, PDA, or smart phone	*Multifunction peripheral; ink-jet color printer; or laser printer (black-and-white or color), label printer, and postage printer*
Mobile	*15.7-inch LCD screen on notebook computer; color LCD screen on Tablet PC, PDA, or smart phone*	Mobile color printer; ink-jet color printer; laser printer for in-office use (black-and-white or color); photo printer
Power	23-inch LCD monitor	*Laser printer (black-and-white or color); plotter or large-format printer; or photo printer; or dye-sublimation printer*

User	Monitor	Printer
Large business	*19- or 21-inch LCD monitor; color LCD screen on Tablet PC, PDA, or smart phone*	High-speed laser printer; color laser printer; line printer; label printer

Things to Think About

Answers will vary.

Puzzle Answer

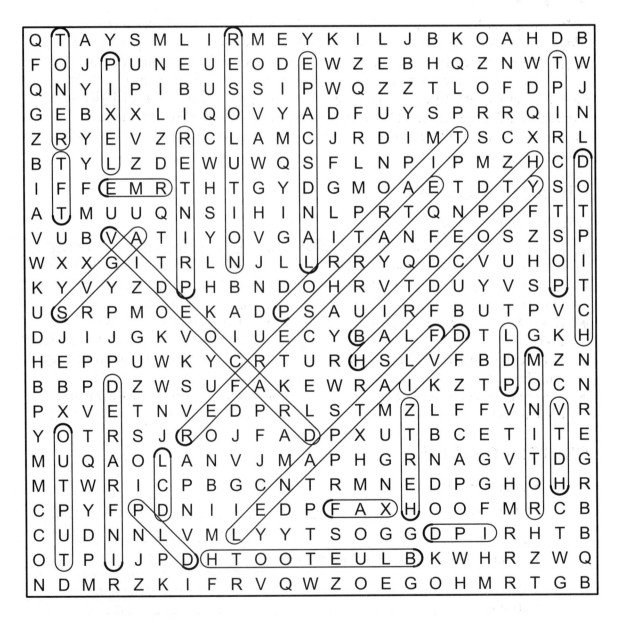

DISCOVERING COMPUTERS 2007

STUDY GUIDE

CHAPTER 7

Storage

Chapter Overview

Storage holds data, instructions, and information, which includes pictures, music, and videos, for future use. Users depend on storage devices to provide access to their storage media for years and decades to come. This chapter identifies and discusses various storage media and storage devices. Storage media covered include internal hard disks, portable hard disks, floppy disks, Zip disks, CD-ROMs, recordable CDs, rewritable CDs, DVD-ROMs, recordable DVDs, rewritable DVDs, tape, PC Cards, flash memory cards, USB flash drives, smart cards, and microfilm and microfiche.

Chapter Objectives

After completing this chapter, you should be able to:

- Differentiate between storage devices and storage media
- Describe the characteristics of magnetic disks
- Describe the characteristics of a hard disk
- Differentiate between floppy disks and Zip disks
- Describe the characteristics of optical discs

- Differentiate among CD-ROMs, recordable CDs, rewritable CDs, DVD-ROMs, recordable DVDs, and rewritable DVDs
- Identify the uses of tape
- Discuss PC Cards and the various types of miniature mobile storage media
- Identify uses of microfilm and microfiche

CHAPTER OUTLINE

I.   Storage [p. 354]

Storage holds _____

_____

A storage medium (or secondary storage) is _____

_____

Capacity is _____

_____

113

A storage device is _____

Writing is _____
_____

Reading is _____
_____

Access time measures _____
_____

Transfer rate is _____
_____

Transfer rates for disks are stated in _____

II. Magnetic disks [p. 357]

Magnetic disks use _____
_____

Formatting is _____

A track is _____

A sector is _____

A cluster (or allocation unit) is _____

The term portable means _____

A. Hard disks [p. 358]

A hard disk, or a hard disk drive, is _____
_____

A fixed disk is _____
_____

Longitudinal recording aligns _____
_____

Perpendicular recording aligns _____
_____

1. Characteristics of a hard disk [p. 359]

A platter is _____
_____

The form factor of platters is _____
_____

A read/write head is _____
_____

A cylinder is _____

The platters spin continually at a high rate of speed, usually 5,400 to 15,000 revolutions per minute (rpm), with the read/write heads floating on a cushion of air just above the platter surface.

A head crash occurs _____

A backup is _____

Disk cache is _____

2. Miniature hard disks [p. 362]

   Many mobile devices and consumer electronics include miniature hard disks, which provide users with greater storage capacities than flash memory, and which have storage capacities that range from _____

   _____

3. Portable hard disks [p. 362]

   An external hard disk is _____

   _____

   A removable hard disk is _____

   _____

4. Hard disk controllers [p. 363]

   A disk controller is _____

   _____

   Types of hard disk controllers for personal computers:

   SATA (Serial Advanced Technology Attachment) uses _____

   _____

   EIDE (Enhanced Integrated Drive Electronics) is _____

   _____

   SCSI interfaces can _____

   _____

5. Maintaining data stored on a hard disk [p. 363]

   To prevent loss of data, you should perform preventative maintenance such as _____

6. Online storage [p. 363]

   Online storage is _____

   Reasons people use online storage service:

   _____

   _____

   _____

B. Floppy disks [p. 364]

A floppy disk (or diskette) is _____

_____

A floppy disk drive is _____

_____

An external floppy disk drive is _____

_____

Density is _____

_____

A disk with a higher density has a larger storage capacity. Most disks today are high density (HD).

A write-protect notch is _____

_____

C. Zip disks [p. 365]

A Zip disk is _____

_____

A Zip drive is _____

_____

III. Optical discs [p. 366]

An optical disc is _____

_____

Mini discs have _____

A. Care of optical discs [p. 368]

A jewel box is _____

Guidelines for proper care of compact discs:

- Do not expose _____

- Do not stack_____

- Do not touch _____

B. Types of optical discs [p. 368]

Many different formats of optical discs exist today. Two general categories are CDs and DVDs, with DVDs having a much greater storage capacity than CDs.

C. CD-ROMs [p. 369]

A CD-ROM, or compact disc read-only memory, is_____

_____

The contents of a standard CD-ROM are recorded by the manufacturer and cannot be erased or modified.

A standard CD-ROM is called a single-session disc because_____

_____

A CD-ROM drive is_____

A CD-ROM can hold_____

The speed of a CD-ROM is_____

_____

CD-ROM drives use an X to denote the original data transfer rate of 150 KB per second (KBps). A 48X CD-ROM drive has a data transfer rate of 7,200 (48 x 150) KBps, or 7.2 MB per second. The higher the data transfer rate, the smoother the playback of images and sounds.

D. Picture CDs [p. 370]

A Picture CD is _____

_____

E. CD-Rs and CD-RWs [p. 371]

A CD-R (compact disc-recordable) is _____

_____

Multisession means _____

A CD-R drive, or CD recorder, is used to_____

_____

A CD-RW (compact disc-rewritable) is _____

_____

A CD-RW drive is used to _____

_____

Burning is _____

_____

Ripping is _____

_____

F. DVD-ROMs [p. 372]

A DVD-ROM (digital versatile disc-ROM or digital video disc-ROM) is_____

_____

Use DVD-video format to _____

A DVD-ROM drive can read _____

_____

A DVD-ROM drive that also can read audio CDs, CD-ROMs, CD-Rs, and CD-RWs is advertised by manufacturers as a CD-RW/DVD.

DVD-ROMs increase storage capacity using one of three storage techniques:

_____

_____

_____

A Blu-Ray disc has _____

The HD-DVD disc has _____

The UMD (Universal Media Disc) can _____

_____

G. Recordable and rewritable DVDs [p. 373]

You can obtain recordable and rewritable versions of DVD.

* DVD-R and DVD+R are _____

_____

* With DVD-RW and DVD+RW you can _____

_____

To write on DVD-RW and DVD+RW disks, you must have a _____

_____

With DVD+RAM (DVD+random access memory), you can _____

_____

IV. Tape [p. 374]

Tape is_____

A tape drive reads _____

A tape cartridge is _____

A tape library is _____

Tape requires sequential access, which refers to _____

_____

Floppy disks, hard disks, and compact discs use direct access, or random access, which means _____

_____

V. PC Cards [p. 374]

    A PC Card is _____

    _____

VI. Miniature mobile storage media [p. 375]

    A digital photo viewer is_____

    A. Flash memory cards [p. 376]

        Solid-state media are _____

        _____

        Common types of flash memory cards include _____

        _____

        A card reader/writer is _____

        _____

    B. USB flash drives [p. 377]

        A USB flash drive (or pen drive) is _____

        _____

    C. Smart cards [p. 378]

        A smart card stores _____

        _____

VII. Microfilm and microfiche [p. 379]

    Microfilm and microfiche store microscopic images of documents.

    Microfilm uses _____

    Microfiche uses _____

    A computer output microfilm recorder is _____

    _____

VIII. Enterprise storage [p. 379]

    To meet their large-scale needs, enterprises use _____

    _____

IX. Putting it all together [p. 380]

    Many factors influence the type of storage devices you should use, including: ___

    _____

    _____

Self Test

Matching

1. ____ hard disk
2. ____ floppy disk
3. ____ Zip disk
4. ____ CD-ROM
5. ____ DVD-ROM
6. ____ tape
7. ____ PC Card
8. ____ USB flash drive
9. ____ smart card
10. ____ microfiche

a. extremely high-capacity compact disc capable of storing from 4.7 GB to 17 GB

b. uses a small sheet of film to store microscopic images of documents

c. portable, inexpensive, flexible storage medium enclosed in a square-shaped plastic shell

d. magnetically coated ribbon capable of storing large amounts of data at a low cost

e. similar in size to a credit card, stores data on a thin microprocessor embedded in the card

f. consists of several inflexible, circular platters that store items magnetically

g. thin, credit-card-sized device that fits into a slot on a notebook or other personal computer

h. sequential access storage medium whose contents are lost when power is turned off

i. a type of portable magnetic media that can store from 100 MB to 750 MB of data

j. lightweight enough to be transported on a keychain; convenient for mobile users

k. temporarily holds data and instructions while they are being processed by the CPU

l. optical disc that uses laser technology to store data and info

True/False

____ 1. Storage holds items such as data, instructions, and information for future use.

____ 2. Even if a file consists of only a few bytes, it uses an entire cluster of a floppy disk for storage.

____ 3. Current personal computer hard disks can store from 80 to 500 GB and more of data, instructions, and information.

____ 4. On desktop computers, platters have a platter factor of approximately 2.5 inches or less.

____ 5. An external hard disk is a hard disk that you insert and remove from a hard disk drive.

_____ 6. One use of online storage is to save time by storing large video and graphics files instantaneously, instead of downloading them to the local hard disk.

_____ 7. On a floppy disk, if the write-protect notch is open, the drive can write on the floppy disk.

_____ 8. A Zip drive can read standard floppy disks as well as Zip disks.

_____ 9. Original CD-ROM drives were single-speed drives with transfer rates of 7.2 MBps.

_____ 10. A Kodak Picture CD is a multisession disc, which means users can save additional photos on the disc at a later time.

Multiple Choice

_____ 1. What is the smallest unit of disk space that stores data?
   a. track
   b. sector
   c. cluster
   d. cylinder

_____ 2. Traditionally, hard disks stored data using what kind of recording?
   a. perpendicular
   b. synchronized
   c. parallel
   d. longitudinal

_____ 3. If a computer has one floppy disk drive, what is it named?
   a. drive A
   b. drive B
   c. drive C
   d. drive D

_____ 4. How much data can a typical floppy disk store?
   a. 1.44 KB (approximately 1.44 thousand bytes)
   b. 1.44 MB (approximately 1.44 million bytes)
   c. 1.44 GB (approximately 1.44 billion bytes)
   d. 1.44 TB (approximately 1.44 trillion bytes)

_____ 5. What should you do to care properly for a compact disc?
   a. hold the disc by its edges
   b. stack discs
   c. touch the underside of the disc
   d. eat, smoke, or drink near the disc

_____ 6. What speed CD-ROM would have a data transfer rate of 7,200 KB or 7.2 MB per second?
   a. 8X
   b. 16X
   c. 32X
   d. 48X

        7. Which of the following is an erasable disc you can write on multiple times?
            a. CD-ER
            b. CD-R
            c. CD-W
            d. CD-RW

        8. What is the maximum storage capacity of current USB flash drives?
            a. 2 GB
            b. 4 GB
            c. 6 GB
            d. 10 GB

        9. Which of the following is a use of smart cards?
            a. tracking customer purchases
            b. authenticating users for Internet purchases
            c. storing vaccination data
            d. all of the above

      10. What do libraries use to store back issues of newspapers, magazines, and genealogy records?
            a. floppy disks and hard disks
            b. CD-ROMs and DVD-ROMs
            c. PC Cards and smart cards
            d. microfilm and microfiche

Fill in the Blanks

1. A storage _____ is the physical material on which a computer keeps data, instructions, and information.

2. _____ is the process of preparing a disk for reading and writing.

3. Sometimes called a(n) _____, the hard disk inside the system unit of most desktop computers is not portable.

4. A(n) _____ occurs when a read/write head touches the surface of a hard disk platter, usually resulting in a loss of data.

5. A(n) _____ is a duplicate of a file, program, or disk that can be used if the original is lost, damaged, or destroyed.

6. _____, the newest type of hard disk interface, uses serial signals to transfer data, instructions, and information.

7. A Kodak _____ is a type of compact disc that stores digital versions of a single roll of film using a jpg file format.

8. A mini-DVD that has grown in popularity is the _____, which works specifically with the PlayStation Portable handheld game console.

9. Three competing rewritable DVD formats exist: DVD+RW, DVD-RW, and _____.

10. Common types of miniature _____ storage media include flash memory cards, USB flash drives, and smart cards.

Complete the Table

OPTICAL DISK FORMATS

Optical Disc	Read?	Write?	Erase?
_____	Y	N	N
CD-R	_____	_____	_____
_____	Y	Y	Y
DVD-ROM	_____	_____	_____
_____ and _____	Y	Y	N
DVD-RW, DVD+RW, and DVD+RAM	_____	_____	_____

Things to Think About

1. How is sequential access different from direct access? Are there any circumstances under which sequential access has an advantage over direct access?

2. Given the advantages of online storage, will it ultimately replace local hard drives and other local storage media? Why or why not?

3. Should recording or movie companies be able to use formatting techniques to keep people from copying CDs or DVDs?

4. Will compact discs, such as CD-ROMs or DVD-ROMs, someday replace magnetic media, such as tape or a floppy disk, or other media, such as microfilm or microfiche? Why or why not?

Puzzle

Use the given clues to complete the crossword puzzle.

Across

4. Small arcs into which a disk's tracks are broken
6. Flat, round, portable metal storage medium, usually 4.75 inches in diameter
7. The newest type of hard disk interface
8. Extremely high capacity compact disc
10. The number of bits in an area on a storage medium
12. Minimum time it takes a storage device to locate an item on a disk
14. Consists of two to eight sectors
15. Controller that can support up to eight or fifteen peripheral devices
17. Made of aluminum, glass, or ceramic; determines a hard disk's capacity
18. Process of preparing a disk for reading and writing by organizing the disk into storage locations
19. Type of protective box for CDs and DVDs
22. A multisession, non-erasable CD onto which users record their own items
23. One of the first storage media used with mainframe computers
24. Thin, credit-card-sized device that fits into a personal computer expansion slot
25. Stores images of documents on roll film
26. Portion of memory the processor uses to store frequently accessed items

Down

1. Silver-colored compact disc that can contain text, graphics, video, and sound
2. Flash memory device that plugs in a USB port on a computer or mobile device
3. Number of bytes a storage medium can hold
4. Holds items such as data, instructions, and information for future use
5. Process of transferring items from a storage medium into memory
9. Duplicate of a file, program, or disk that can be used if the original is lost
11. Narrow recording band that forms a full circle on a disk surface
13. Stores images of documents on sheet film
16. Process of transferring items from memory to a storage medium
18. Portable, inexpensive storage medium
20. One of the more widely used controllers for hard disks
21. Occurs when a read/write head touches the surface of a hard disk platter

Self Test Answers

Matching

1. *f* [p. 358]
2. *c* [p. 364]
3. *i* [p. 365]
4. *l* [p. 369]
5. *a* [p. 372]
6. *d* [p. 374]
7. *g* [p. 374]
8. *j* [p. 377]
9. *e* [p. 378]
10. *b* [p. 379]

True/False

1. *T* [p. 354]
2. *T* [p. 357]
3. *T* [p. 358]
4. *F* [p. 360]
5. *F* [p. 362]
6. *T* [p. 364]
7. *F* [p. 365]
8. *F* [p. 365]
9. *F* [p. 369]
10. *F* [p. 370]

Multiple Choice

1. *c* [p. 357]
2. *d* [p. 358]
3. *a* [p. 365]
4. *b* [p. 365]
5. *a* [p. 368]
6. *d* [p. 369]
7. *d* [p. 371]
8. *b* [p. 377]
9. *d* [p. 378]
10. *d* [p. 379]

Fill in the Blanks

1. *medium* [p. 355]
2. *Formatting* [p. 357]
3. *fixed disk* [p. 358]
4. *head crash* [p. 360]
5. *backup* [p. 361]
6. *SATA* or *Serial Advanced Technology Attachment* [p. 363]
7. *Picture CD* [p. 370]
8. *UMD (Universal Media Disc)* [p. 372]
9. *DVD+RAM* [p. 373]
10. *mobile* [p. 375]

Complete the Table

OPTICAL DISC FORMATS

Optical Disc	Read?	Write?	Erase?
CD-ROM	Y	N	N
CD-R	*Y*	*Y*	*N*
CD-RW	Y	Y	Y
DVD-ROM	*Y*	*N*	*N*
DVD-R and *DVD+R*	Y	Y	N
DVD-RW, DVD+RW, and DVD+RAM	*Y*	*Y*	*Y*

Things to Think About

Answers will vary.

Puzzle Answer

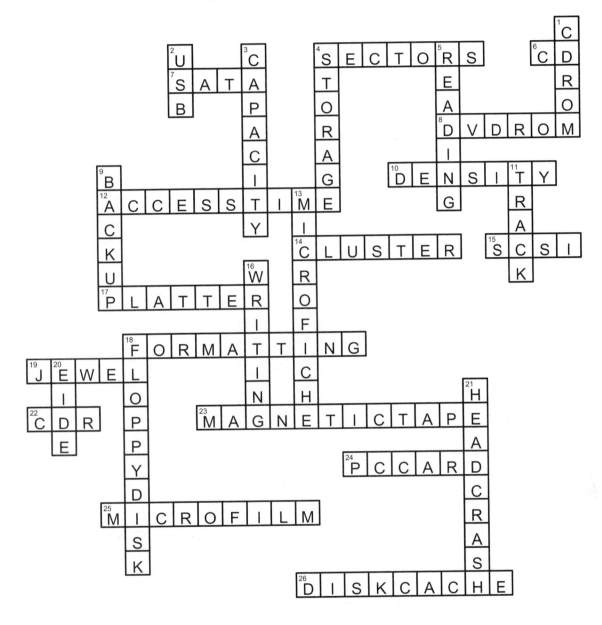

Notes

DISCOVERING COMPUTERS 2007
STUDY GUIDE

CHAPTER 8

Operating Systems and Utility Programs

Chapter Overview

This chapter defines an operating system and then discusses the functions common to most operating systems. Next, it introduces several utility programs commonly found in operating systems. The chapter discusses a variety of stand-alone operating systems, network operating systems, and embedded operating systems. Finally, the chapter describes several stand-alone utility programs.

Chapter Objectives

After completing this chapter, you should be able to:

- Identify the types of system software
- Summarize the startup process on a personal computer
- Describe the functions of an operating system
- Discuss ways that some operating systems help administrators control a network and administer security
- Explain the purpose of the utilities included with most operating systems
- Summarize the features of several stand-alone operating systems
- Identify various network operating systems
- Identify devices that use several embedded operating systems
- Explain the purpose of several stand-alone utility programs

Chapter Outline

I. System software [p. 398]

System software consists of _____

_____

II. Operating systems [p. 398]

An operating system (OS) is_____

_____

The operating system sometimes is called the _____

A cross-platform program is _____

_____

III. Operating system functions [p. 400]

Most operating systems provide similar functions.

A. Starting a computer [p. 400]

Booting is _____

_____

- A cold boot is _____
- A warm boot is _____

The kernel is _____

The kernel is a memory resident program, which means _____

_____

Nonresident parts of the OS are _____

_____

Steps in a cold boot using the Windows XP operating system:

1. _____

_____

2. _____

_____

The BIOS (basic input/output system) is _____

3. _____

_____

The POST (power-on self test) check _____

_____

4. _____

_____

5. _____

_____

System files are _____

6. _____

_____

7. _____

_____

The registry consists of _____

_____

The Startup folder contains _____

_____

1. Recovery disk [p. 402]

    A boot drive is _____

    _____

    A recovery (or boot) disk is _____

    _____

B. Providing a user interface [p. 402]

    A user interface controls _____

    _____

    1. Command-line interface [p. 402]

        With a command-line interface, you type _____

        _____

        A command language is _____

        Scripts are _____

    2. Menu-driven interface [p. 402]

        A menu-driven interface provides _____

        _____

    3. Graphical user interface [p. 402]

        A graphical user interface (GUI) allows _____

        _____

C. Managing programs [p. 403]

    • A single user/single tasking operating system allows _____

    _____

    • A single user/multitasking operating system allows _____

    _____

    The foreground contains _____

    The background contains _____

    • Preemptive multitasking is _____

    _____

    • A multiuser operating system enables _____

    _____

    • A multiprocessing operating system supports _____

    _____

    A fault-tolerant computer continues _____

    _____

D. Managing memory [p. 405]

The purpose of memory management is _____

_____

With virtual memory, the operating system allocates _____

_____

- A swap file is _____
- A page is _____
- Paging is _____
- Thrashing is _____

E. Scheduling jobs [p. 406]

A job is _____

A buffer is _____

Spooling is _____

Multiple print jobs line up in a(n) _____

A print spooler intercepts _____

F. Configuring devices [p. 407]

A driver, short for device driver, is_____

_____

Plug and Play means _____

_____

An interrupt request line (IRQ) is _____

_____

G. Establishing an Internet connection [p. 409]

Operating systems typically provide a means to establish Internet connections. Some operating systems include a Web browser and an e-mail program.

H. Monitoring performance [p. 409]

A performance monitor is_____

_____

I. Providing file management and other utilities [p. 410]

Some of the capabilities with which operating systems often provide users include: _____

_____

J. Controlling a network [410]

A network operating system (or network OS) is _____

_____

The network administrator uses _____

_____

K. Administering security [p. 410]

To log on, or access, a network, you must have a user name and password.

- A user name (or user ID) is _____
- A password is _____

Encryption is _____

_____

IV. Operating system utility programs [p. 411]

A utility, or utility program, is _____

_____

Utility programs provide a variety of functions, including: _____

_____

A. File manager [p. 412]

A file manager is_____

_____

Windows XP includes a file manager called _____

A shortcut is _____

_____

Formatting is _____

_____

B. Image viewer [p. 412]

An image viewer is _____

_____

Windows XP includes an image viewer called _____

C. Personal firewall [p. 413]

A personal firewall is _____

_____

A hacker is _____

D. Uninstaller [p. 413]

An uninstaller is _____

_____

E. Disk scanner [p. 414]

A disk scanner is _____

_____

F. Disk defragmenter [p. 414]

A disk defragmenter is _____

_____

A fragmented file is _____

_____

Defragmenting a disk stores files in _____

_____

G. Diagnostic utility [p. 414]

A diagnostic utility is _____

_____

Dr. Watson is used to _____

_____

H. Backup utility [p. 415]

A backup utility allows _____

_____

To compress a file means _____

A restore program reverses _____

_____

I. Screen saver [p. 415]

A screen saver is _____

_____

Ghosting is _____

_____

V. Types of operating systems [p. 415]

Many early operating systems were device dependent and proprietary, but the
trend today is towards device-independent operating systems.

• Device-dependent programs run _____

_____

Proprietary software is _____

• Device-independent operating systems run _____

_____

Service packs provide _____

_____

VI. Stand-alone operating systems [p. 416]

A stand-alone operating system is _____

Client operating systems can operate _____

_____

A. DOS [p. 417]

   DOS (Disk Operating System) refers to _____

   _____

   Developed by Microsoft, DOS used a command-line interface. At one time, DOS was a widely used operating system.

B. Windows XP [p. 417]

   Windows XP is _____

   _____

   Windows XP is available in five editions.

   Windows XP Home Edition offers _____

   _____

   Windows XP Professional includes _____

   _____

   Windows XP Media Center Edition includes _____

   _____

   A Media Center PC is _____

   Windows XP Tablet PC Edition includes _____

   _____

   The Windows XP 64-bit Edition is designed for _____

   _____

C. Windows Vista [p. 419]

   Windows Vista is _____

   _____

   Windows Vista is available in several editions, which are grouped into two general categories: _____

D. Mac OS X [p. 420]

   Apple's Macintosh operating system has set _____

   _____

   Mac OS X is _____

   Features of Mac OS X include _____

   _____

E. UNIX [p. 420]

UNIX is _____

_____

F. Linux [p. 421]

Linux is _____

_____

Open source software is _____

_____

VII. Network operating systems [p. 422]

A network operating system is designed specifically to support a network.

A. NetWare [p. 422]

NetWare is _____

_____

B. Windows Server 2003 [p. 422]

Windows Server 2003 is _____

_____

Windows Server 2003 offers a central information repository about network
users and resources with _____

The Windows Server 2003 family includes:

- _____   • _____
- _____   • _____
- _____

Windows Server System provides _____

Through Windows Server 2003, programs have the ability to use Web
services, which are _____

C. UNIX [p. 423]

UNIX is capable of _____

_____

UNIX is a multipurpose operating system because _____

_____

D. Linux [p. 423]

Linux is _____

_____

    E. Solaris [p. 423]

       Solaris is _____

       _____

VIII. Embedded operating systems [p. 423]

     An embedded operating system resides _____

     _____

    A. Windows CE [p. 423]

       Windows CE is _____

       _____

    B. Windows Mobile [p. 424]

       Windows Mobile is _____

       _____

       A Pocket PC is _____

    C. Palm OS [p. 424]

       Palm OS is _____

       _____

    D. Embedded Linux [p. 425]

       Embedded Linux is _____

       _____

    E. Symbian OS [p. 425]

       Symbian OS is _____

       _____

  IX. Stand-alone utility programs [p. 425]

     The functions of a stand-alone utility program include _____

     _____

    A. Antivirus programs [p. 425]

       A virus is _____

       A virus author is _____

       _____

       Malware is _____

       _____

       A worm is _____

       _____

       A Trojan horse is _____

       _____

An antivirus program is _____

_____

B. Spyware removers [p. 426]

Spyware is _____

_____

Adware is _____

_____

A spyware remover is _____

_____

C. Internet filters [p. 426]

Filters are _____

_____

1. Anti-spam programs [p. 426]

Spam is _____

_____

An anti-spam program is _____

_____

2. Web filters [p. 427]

Web filtering software is _____

_____

3. Pop-up blockers [p. 427]

A pop-up ad is _____

_____

A pop-up blocker is _____

_____

D. File conversion [p. 427]

A file conversion utility transforms _____

_____

E. File compression [p. 427]

A file compression utility shrinks _____

_____

Zipped files are _____

To uncompress, or unzip, a file, you _____

F. CD/DVD burning [p. 428]

CD/DVD burning software writes _____

_____

G. Personal computer maintenance [p. 428]

A personal computer maintenance utility is _____

_____

Self Test

Matching

1. _____ file manager
2. _____ image viewer
3. _____ uninstaller
4. _____ disk scanner
5. _____ disk defragmenter
6. _____ diagnostic utility
7. _____ screen saver
8. _____ Web filtering software
9. _____ pop-up blocker
10. _____ file compression utility

a. stops pop-up ads from displaying on Web pages

b. utility that permanently etches images on a monitor screen

c. Windows Explorer, in Windows XP

d. reduces the size of a file so it takes up less storage space than the original file

e. utility that detects and corrects disk problems and searches for and removes unwanted files

f. utility that causes the screen to display a moving image after a period of inactivity

g. allows users to display and copy the contents of a graphics file

h. compiles technical information about a computer's hardware and prepares a report

i. restricts access to certain material on the Web

j. utility that removes a program, as well as associated entries in the system files

k. utility that locates, indexes, and loads system configuration information

l. utility that reorganizes files and unused space on a computer's hard disk

True/False

_____ 1. With Windows XP, you can perform a warm boot by clicking the Start button on the taskbar, clicking Turn Off Computer on the Start menu, and then clicking Restart in the Turn off computer dialog box.

_____ 2. During the boot process, if the system files are not on a disk in drive A or on a disc in a CD or DVD drive, the BIOS looks in drive C (the designation usually given to the first hard disk).

_____ 3. With a multitasking operating system, the application you currently are working on is in the background, and the others that are running but not being used are in the foreground.

_____ 4. To stop thrashing, you should quit the application that stopped responding.

_____ 5. With spooling, multiple print jobs are queued, or lined up, in the buffer.

_____ 6. If you add a new device to your computer, such as a printer, its driver must be installed before the device will be operational.

_____ 7. When the contents of a file are gathered across two or more contiguous sectors on a disk, the file is fragmented.

_____ 8. The disadvantage of device-independent operating systems is that if you change computer models or vendors, you cannot retain existing application software files and data files.

_____ 9. Today, DOS is widely used because it offers a graphical user interface and can take full advantage of modern 32-bit personal computer processors.

_____ 10. Because only one version exists, UNIX provides interoperability across multiple platforms.

Multiple Choice

_____ 1. What is the core of the operating system called?
   a. boot
   b. registry
   c. kernel
   d. BIOS

_____ 2. Today, what are most operating systems?
   a. single user/single tasking
   b. multitasking
   c. multiuser
   d. multiprocessing

_____ 3. Swap files, pages, paging, and thrashing all are terms related to what basic function of an operating system?
   a. managing memory
   b. configuring devices
   c. monitoring system performance
   d. administering security

_____ 4. What is the program that manages and intercepts print jobs and places them in the queue called?
   a. print driver
   b. print spooler
   c. print buffer
   d. print saver

_____ 5. What multitasking operating system is available only for computers manufactured by Apple?
   a. Linux
   b. UNIX
   c. Windows Vista
   d. Mac OS X

_____ 6. Which of the following is open source software?
  a. UNIX
  b. Windows XP
  c. Linux
  d. all of the above

_____ 7. Which of the following is capable of being both a stand-alone operating system and a network operating system?
  a. UNIX
  b. Solaris
  c. Windows Server 2003
  d. NetWare

_____ 8. Which of the following is *not* a network operating system?
  a. Symbian OS
  b. Linux
  c. Solaris
  d. UNIX

_____ 9. Which of the following is *not* an embedded operating system?
  a. Palm OS
  b. Windows CE
  c. UNIX
  d. Symbian OS

_____ 10. Which of the following does *not* replicate itself to other computers?
  a. virus
  b. worm
  c. Trojan horse
  d. none of the above

Fill in the Blanks

1. Parts of an operating system are _____, which means their instructions remain on the hard disk until they are needed.

2. If the POST completes successfully, the BIOS searches for specific operating system files called _____.

3. A(n) _____ continues to operate even if one of its components fails.

4. With _____, the operating system allocates a portion of a storage medium, usually the hard disk, to function as additional RAM.

5. A(n) _____ is a segment of memory or storage in which items are placed while waiting to be transferred from an input device or to an output device.

6. A(n) _____ is a program that assesses and reports information about various computer resources and devices.

7. A personal _____ is a utility program that detects and protects a personal computer from unauthorized intrusions.

8. Screen savers were developed to prevent a problem called _____, in which images could be permanently etched on a monitor's screen.

9. Windows _____ is Microsoft's fastest, most reliable and efficient operating system to date.

10. _____ is an unsolicited e-mail message or newsgroup posting sent to many recipients or newsgroups at once.

Complete the Table

CATEGORIES OF OPERATING SYSTEMS

Category	Operating System Name
Stand-alone	• DOS
	• Early Windows versions (Windows 3.x, Windows 95, Windows NT Workstation, Windows 98, Windows 2000 Professional, Windows Millennium Edition)
	• _____
	• _____
	• Mac OS X
	• UNIX
	• _____
_____	• _____
	• Early Windows Server versions (Windows NT Server, Windows 2000 Server)
	• _____
	• _____
	• Linux
	• _____
Embedded	• _____
	• Windows Mobile
	• _____
	• _____
	• Symbian OS

Things to Think About

1. How has the concept of user-friendly (being easy to learn and use) affected the development of operating systems? What operating systems seem the most, and least, user-friendly? Why?

2. Why is a boot disk important? In Windows, how can you create a boot disk?

3. What three functions of an operating system are most important for a home computer user? For an office computer user? Why?

4. From most important to least important, how would you rank the utility programs described in this chapter? Why did you rank the programs as you did?

Puzzle

The terms described by the phrases below are written below each line in code. Break the code by writing the correct term above the coded word. Then, use your broken code to translate the final sentence.

1. Consists of the programs that control the operations of the computer and its devices

   OUOPAI OKBPSWNA

2. A set of programs containing instructions that coordinate all of the activities among hardware

   KLANWPEJC OUOPAI

3. Firmware that contains the computer's startup instructions

   XEKO

4. Dr. Watson is an example of this kind of utility

   ZEWCJKOPEY

5. Microsoft's fastest, most reliable, and efficient Windows operating system to date

   SEJZKSO REOPW

6. A small image that represents an item such as a program, an instruction, or a file

   EYKJ

7. Operating system capability that allows a user to work on two or more applications that reside in memory

   IQHPEPWOGEJC

8. Allocates a portion of a storage medium to function as additional RAM

   RENPQWH IAIKNU

9. What happens when an operating system spends too much time paging instead of executing software

   PDNWODEJC

10. Small program that converts commands into instructions a hardware device understands

    ZNERAN

11. A communications line between a device and the CPU

    EJPANNQLP NAMQAOP

12. Combination of characters associated with a user name that allows access to certain computer resources

    LWOOSKNZ

13. Program that performs functions related to storage and file management

    BEHA IWJWCAN

14. Turning on a computer after it has been powered off completely

    YKHZ XKKP

15. Several files in which the system configuration information is contained

    NACEOPNU

16. Floppy disk that contains certain operating system commands that will start the computer

    XKKP ZEOG

17. A type of system software that performs a specific task, usually related to managing a computer

   QPEHEPU LNKCNWI

18. Compressed files, usually with a .zip extension

   VELLAZ BEHAO

19. What you do to restore a zipped file to its original form

   QJYKILNAOO

20. Windows XP utility that reorganizes a disk so files are stored in contiguous sectors

   ZEOG ZABNWCIAJPAN

W LNKCNWI YWHHAZ OUOPAI YKIIWJZAN 8.0 IWGAO

YDKKOEJC WJ KLANWPEJC OUOPAI AWOEAN XU AHEIEJWPEJC PDA

JAAZ PK IWGA W YDKEYA, WHHKSEJC QOANO PK OSEPYD AWOEHU

WIKJC QL PK PDENPU-PSK ZEBBANAJP KLANWPEJC OUOPAIO.

Self Test Answers

Matching	True/False	Multiple Choice	Fill in the Blanks
1. *c* [p. 412]	1. *T* [p. 400]	1. *c* [p. 400]	1. *nonresident* [p. 400]
2. *g* [p. 412]	2. *T* [p. 401]	2. *b* [p. 403]	2. *system files* [p. 401]
3. *j* [p. 413]	3. *F* [p. 404]	3. *a* [p. 406]	3. *fault-tolerant computer* [p. 405]
4. *e* [p. 414]	4. *T* [p. 406]	4. *b* [p. 407]	4. *virtual memory* [p. 406]
5. *l* [p. 414]	5. *T* [p. 407]	5. *d* [p. 420]	5. *buffer* [p. 407]
6. *h* [p. 414]	6. *T* [p. 407]	6. *c* [p. 421]	6. *performance monitor* [p. 409]
7. *f* [p. 415]	7. *F* [p. 414]	7. *a* [p. 422]	7. *firewall* [p. 413]
8. *i* [p. 427]	8. *F* [p. 416]	8. *a* [p. 422]	8. *ghosting* [p. 415]
9. *a* [p. 427]	9. *F* [p. 417]	9. *c* [p. 425]	9. *Vista* [p. 419]
10. *d* [p. 427]	10. *F* [p. 420]	10. *c* [p. 426]	10. *spam* [p. 426]

Complete the Table

CATEGORIES OF OPERATING SYSTEMS

Category	Operating System Name
Stand-alone	• DOS • Early Windows versions (Windows 3.x, Windows 95, Windows NT Workstation, Windows 98, Windows 2000 Professional, Windows Millennium Edition) • *Windows XP* • *Windows Vista* • Mac OS X • UNIX • *Linux*
Network	• *NetWare* • Early Windows Server versions (Windows NT Server, Windows 2000 Server) • *Windows Server 2003* • *UNIX* • Linux • *Solaris*
Embedded	• *Windows CE* • Windows Mobile • *Palm OS* • *Embedded Linux* • Symbian OS

Things to Think About

Answers will vary.

Puzzle Answer

1. Consists of the programs that control the operations of the computer and its devices

   system software
   OUOPAI OKBPSWNA

2. A set of programs containing instructions that coordinate all of the activities among hardware

   operating system
   KLANWPEJC OUOPAI

3. Firmware that contains the computer's startup instructions

   BIOS
   XEKO

4. Dr. Watson is an example of this kind of utility

   diagnostic
   ZEWCJKOPEY

5. Microsoft's fastest, most reliable, and efficient Windows operating system to date

   Windows Vista
   SEJZKSO REOPW

6. A small image that represents an item such as a program, an instruction, or a file

   icon
   EYKJ

7. Operating system capability that allows a user to work on two or more applications that reside in memory

   multitasking
   IQHPEPWOGEJC

8. Allocates a portion of a storage medium to function as additional RAM

   virtual memory
   RENPQWH IAIKNU

9. What happens when an operating system spends too much time paging instead of executing software

   thrashing
   PDNWODEJC

10. Small program that converts commands into instructions a hardware device understands

    driver
    ZNERAN

11. A communications line between a device and the CPU

    interrupt request
    EJPANNQLP NAMQAOP

12. Combination of characters associated with a user name that allows access to certain computer resources

    password
    LWOOSKNZ

13. Program that performs functions related to storage and file management

    file manager
    BEHA IWJWCAN

14. Turning on a computer after it has been powered off completely

    cold boot
    YKHZ XKKP

15. Several files in which the system configuration information is contained

    registry
    NACEOPNU

16. Floppy disk that contains certain operating system commands that will start the computer

    boot disk
    XKKP ZEOG

17. A type of system software that performs a specific task, usually related to managing a computer

    utility program
    QPEHEPU LNKCNWI

18. Compressed files, usually with a .zip extension

    zipped files
    VELLAZ BEHAO

19. What you do to restore a zipped file to its original form

    uncompress
    QJYKILNAOO

20. Windows XP utility that reorganizes a disk so files are stored in contiguous sectors

    disk defragmenter
    ZEOG ZABNWCIAJPAN

A program called System Commander 8.0 makes

W LNKCNWI YWHHAZ OUOPAI YKIIWJZAN 8.0 IWGAO

choosing an operating system easier by eliminating the

YDKKOEJC WJ KLANWPEJC OUOPAI AWOEAN XU AHEIEJWPEJC PDA

need to make a choice, allowing users to switch easily

JAAZ PK IWGA W YDKEYA, WHHKSEJC QOANO PK OSEPYD AWOEHU

among up to 40 different operating systems.

WIKJC QL PK 40 ZEBBANAJP KLANWPEJC OUOPAIO.

DISCOVERING COMPUTERS 2007

STUDY GUIDE

CHAPTER 9

Communications and Networks

Chapter Overview

This chapter provides an overview of communications terminology and applications. It discusses how to join computers into a network, allowing them to communicate and share resources such as hardware, software, data, and information. The chapter also explains various communications devices, media, and procedures as they relate to computers.

Chapter Objectives

After completing this chapter, you should be able to:

- ◆ Discuss the components required for successful communications
- ◆ Identify various sending and receiving devices
- ◆ Describe uses of computer communications
- ◆ List advantages of using a network
- ◆ Differentiate among client/server, peer-to-peer, and P2P networks
- ◆ Describe the various network communications technologies

- ◆ Explain the purpose of communications software
- ◆ Describe various types of lines for communications over the telephone network
- ◆ Describe commonly used communications devices
- ◆ Discuss different ways to set up a home network
- ◆ Identify various physical and wireless transmission media

Chapter Outline

I. Communications [p. 460]

Computer communications describes _____

_____

For successful communications, you need:

- • A sending device that initiates _____

_____

- • A communications device that connects the sending device to a communications channel.

- A communications channel on which _____
- A communications device that connects the communications channel to a receiving device.
- A receiving device that accepts _____

_____

II. Uses of computer communications [p. 462]

   A. Internet, Web, e-mail, instant messaging, chat rooms, newsgroups, Internet telephony, FTP, Web folders, video conferencing, and fax [p. 462]

    In the course of a day, it is likely you use, or use information generated by, one of these communications technologies.

   B. Wireless messaging services [p. 462]

    The type of messaging you use depends primarily on the services offered by the wireless Internet service provider that works with your cellular phone or PDA.

    1. Text messaging [p. 463]

      Text messaging or SMS (short message service) allows _____

      _____

    2. Wireless instant messaging [p. 463]

      Wireless instant messaging (IM) is_____

      _____

    3. Picture messaging [p. 464]

      Picture messaging or MMS (multimedia message service) is _____

      _____

      Video messaging refers to _____

      _____

   C. Wireless Internet access points [p. 464]

    Wireless Internet access points allow _____

    _____

    A hot spot is _____

    _____

    A 3G network uses _____

    _____

   D. Cybercafés [p. 465]

    A cybercafé is _____

    _____

E. Global positioning system [p. 466]

A global positioning system (GPS) is _____

_____

A GPS receiver is _____

_____

F. Collaboration [p. 467]

Many communications software products provide a means to collaborate (or work online) with other users connected to a server.

An online meeting allows _____

_____

A document management system provides for _____

_____

G. Groupware [p. 468]

Groupware is _____

_____

Workgroup computing includes _____

_____

H. Voice mail [p. 468]

Voice mail allows _____

_____

A voice mailbox is _____

_____

I. Web services [p. 468]

Web services are _____

_____

XML is used to _____

_____

III. Networks [p. 469]

A network is _____

_____

Advantages of using a network:

• Facilitating communications — _____

_____

• Sharing hardware — _____

_____

- Sharing data and information — _____

  _____

  EDI (electronic data interchange) is _____

  _____

- Sharing software — _____

  _____

  A network license is _____
  A site license is _____

- Transferring funds — _____

  _____

  Electronic funds transfer (EFT) is _____

  _____

A value-added network (VAN) is _____

_____

A. LANs, MANs, and WANs [p. 470]
  1. LAN [p. 471]
     A local area network (LAN) is _____

     _____

     A node is _____

     _____

     A wireless LAN (WLAN) is _____

     _____

  2. MAN [p. 472]
     A metropolitan area network (MAN) is _____

     _____

  3. WAN [p. 472]
     A wide area network (WAN) is _____

     _____

     The Internet is the world's largest WAN.
B. Network architectures [p. 472]
Network architecture is _____
  1. Client/server [p. 472]
     A client/server network is _____

     _____

     A server (or host computer) controls _____

     _____

Clients are _____

_____

Dedicated servers perform _____

_____

- A file server stores _____
- A print server manages _____
- A database server stores _____
- A network server manages _____

2. Peer-to-peer [p. 473]

A peer-to-peer network is _____

_____

A peer has _____

_____

3. Internet peer-to-peer [p. 473]

An Internet peer-to-peer (also called P2P or file sharing) network is _____

_____

C. Network topologies [p. 474]

A network topology is _____

_____

Commonly used network topologies are bus, ring, and star.

1. Bus network [p. 474]

A bus network consists of _____

_____

The bus is _____

2. Ring network [p. 474]

In a ring network, a cable forms _____

_____

3. Star network [p. 475]

On a star network, all devices connect _____

_____

The hub is _____

D. Intranets [p. 475]

An intranet is _____

An extranet allows _____

_____

IV. Network communications standards [p. 476]

A network standard defines _____

_____

A protocol is _____

_____

A. Ethernet [p. 476]

Ethernet is _____

_____

- Fast Ethernet transmits _____
- Gigabit Ethernet provides _____
- The 10-Gigabit Ethernet standard supports _____

_____

B. Token ring [p. 476]

The token ring standard specifies _____

_____

A token is _____

_____

C. TCP/IP [p. 477]

TCP/IP (Transmission Control Protocol/Internet Protocol) is _____

_____

- Packets are _____
- Packet switching is _____

D. 802.11 (Wi-Fi) [p. 478]

802.11 is _____

802.11g has _____

802.11n uses _____

An 802.11i network standard specifies _____

_____

The 802.11 standard is often called the _____

_____

Wi-Fi (wireless fidelity) identifies _____

_____

Some cities are set up as a Wi-Fi mesh network, which means _____

_____

E. Bluetooth [p. 478]

Bluetooth is _____

_____

F. IrDA [p. 478]

The IrDA specification is used to _____

A line-of-sight transmission is _____

_____

G. RFID [p. 479]

RFID (radio frequency identification) is _____

_____

H. WiMAX [p. 479]

WiMAX (Worldwide Interoperability for Microwave Access), also known as

802.16, is _____

_____

I. WAP [p. 480]

The Wireless Application Protocol (WAP) specifies _____

_____

V. Communications software [p. 480]

Communications software consists of _____

_____

_____

VI. Communications over the telephone network [p. 481]

The public switched telephone network (PSTN) is _____

_____

Data can be sent over the telephone network using dial-up lines or dedicated lines.

A. Dial-up lines [p. 481]

A dial-up line is _____

_____

B. Dedicated lines [p. 482]

A dedicated line is _____

_____

Popular types of dedicated lines are ISDN lines, DSL, T-carrier lines, and ATM.

C. ISDN lines [p. 482]

ISDN (Integrated Services Digital Network) is _____

Multiplexing is _____

D. DSL [p. 482]

DSL (Digital Subscriber Line) transmits _____

ADSL (asymmetric digital subscriber line) is _____

- The downstream rate is _____
- The upstream rate is _____

E. T-carrier lines [p. 483]

A T-carrier line is _____

- A T1 line is _____

  With a fractional T1, users share _____

- A T3 line is _____

F. ATM [p. 483]

ATM (Asynchronous Transfer Mode) is _____

VII. Communications devices [p. 484]

A communications device is _____

An analog signal consists of _____

A digital signal consists of _____

A. Dial-up modems [p. 485]

A modem, or dial-up modem, converts _____

To modulate means _____

To demodulate means _____

B. ISDN and DSL modems [p. 485]

- A digital modem is _____

- An ISDN modem sends _____

_____

A DSL modem sends _____

_____

C. Cable modems [p. 485]

A cable (or broadband) modem is _____

_____

D. Wireless modems [p. 486]

A wireless modem allows _____

_____

E. Network cards [p. 486]

A network card, sometimes called a network interface card (NIC), is _____

_____

A wireless network card is _____

_____

F. Wireless access points [p. 487]

A wireless access point is _____

_____

G. Routers [p. 488]

A router is _____

_____

A hardware firewall is _____

_____

H. Connecting networks [p. 488]

A hub is _____

VIII. Home networks [p. 489]

A home network is _____

_____

An intelligent home network extends _____

_____

A. Wired home networks [p. 489]

1. Ethernet [p. 489]

An Ethernet network requires _____

_____

2. Powerline cable network [p. 489]

A home powerline cable network is _____

_____

3. Phoneline network [p. 489]

A phoneline network is _____

_____

B. Wireless home networks [p. 490]

A HomeRF (radio frequency) network uses _____

_____

A Wi-Fi network sends _____

_____

IX. Communications channel [p. 491]

Bandwidth is _____

_____

Latency is _____

_____

Transmission media consists of _____

_____

- Baseband media can transmit _____
- Broadband media can transmit _____

Transmission media are one of two types:

- Physical transmission media use _____

_____

- Wireless transmission media send _____

_____

X. Physical transmission media [p. 492]

A. Twisted-pair cable [p. 493]

Twisted-pair cable consists of _____

_____

- Each twisted-pair wire consists of _____

_____

Wires are twisted to reduce noise, which is _____

_____

B. Coaxial cable [p. 493]

Coaxial cable (referred to as coax) consists of _____

_____

_____

C. Fiber-optic cable [p. 493]

Fiber-optic cable consists of _____

_____

An optical fiber is _____

Advantages of fiber-optic cable:

- _____
- _____
- _____
- _____
- _____

Disadvantages of fiber-optic cable are that it costs more than twisted-pair or coaxial cable and can be difficult to install and modify.

XI. Wireless transmission media [p. 494]

A. Infrared [p. 494]

Infrared (IR) is _____

_____

B. Broadcast radio [p. 494]

Broadcast radio is _____

_____

C. Cellular radio [p. 494]

Cellular radio is _____

_____

Several categories of cellular transmissions exist:

- 1G: _____
- 2G: _____
- 3G: _____

GSM (Global System for Mobile Communications), UMTS (Universal Mobile Telecommunications System), GPRS (General Packet Radio Service), and CDMA (Code Division Multiple Access) are 3G standards that allow users to display multimedia and graphics quickly, browse the Web, and transfer data, for example, on a cellular device.

Personal Communications Services (PCS) is _____

_____

D. Microwaves [p. 495]

Microwaves are _____

Fixed wireless involves _____

_____

A microwave station is _____

_____

E. Communications satellite [p. 496]

A communications satellite is _____

_____

- An uplink is _____
- A downlink is _____

Self Test

Matching

1. _____ SMS
2. _____ MMS
3. _____ hot spot
4. _____ cybercafé
5. _____ global positioning system
6. _____ online meeting
7. _____ groupware
8. _____ voice mail
9. _____ Web services
10. _____ XML

a. an area with the capability of wireless Internet connectivity

b. a coffee house or restaurant that provides computers with Internet access to its customers

c. allows participants to share documents with others in real time

d. handheld device that provides access to the Internet from any location

e. includes activities such as shopping, banking, investing, and other uses of electronic money

f. consists of earth-based receivers that accept and analyze satellite signals to determine location

g. standardized tools that enable programmers to create applications that can run on the Internet or an internal business network

h. another name for picture messaging

i. a means for mobile device users to send and receive brief text messages on their devices

j. functions like an answering machine, allowing callers to leave a voice message

k. software application that helps people work together and share information over a network

l. used to format files for Web services

True/False

_____ 1. A receiving device initiates an instruction to transmit data, instructions, or information.

_____ 2. Devices that access a WLAN must have either built-in wireless capability or wireless network cards, PC Cards, or flash cards.

_____ 3. Often, nodes (computers or devices) are connected to a LAN via cables.

_____ 4. In a peer-to-peer network, the server contains both the network operating system and application software.

_____ 5. Two examples of networking software that allow P2P are BitTorrent and Gnutella.

_____ 6. With TCP/IP, packets travel along the fastest available path to a recipient's computer via devices called routers.

_____ 7. Wi-Fi and Bluetooth are competing technologies.

_____ 8. An analog signal consists of individual electrical pulses that represent bits grouped together into bytes.

_____ 9. A home powerline cable network requires additional wiring.

_____ 10. Most of today's computer networks use coaxial cable because other transmission media transmit signals at slower rates.

Multiple Choice

_____ 1. Which of the following uses *no* physical wires?
  a. LAN
  b. MAN
  c. WAN
  d. WLAN

_____ 2. What simple, inexpensive network typically connects fewer than 10 computers together?
  a. file sharing network
  b. client/server network
  c. peer-to-peer network
  d. all of the above

_____ 3. Which of the following are commonly used network topologies?
  a. client/server, peer-to-peer, and P2P
  b. LAN, MAN, and WAN
  c. bus, ring, and star
  d. Ethernet, token ring, and 802.11

_____ 4. What is the most popular network standard for LANs?
  a. Ethernet
  b. 802.11
  c. token ring
  d. Bluetooth

_____ 5. What communications technology commonly is used for Internet transmissions?
  a. TCP/IP
  b. 802.11
  c. IrDA
  d. WAP (Wireless Application Protocol)

_____ 6. With ISDN, the same telephone line that could carry only one computer signal, now can carry three or more signals at once using what technique?
    a. modulating
    b. routing
    c. multiplexing
    d. receiving

_____ 7. Which of the following sometimes is called a broadband modem?
    a. ISDN modem
    b. cable modem
    c. DSL modem
    d. dial-up modem

_____ 8. What do personal computers on a LAN typically contain?
    a. DSL (digital subscriber line)
    b. PCS (personal communications service)
    c. TCP (transmission control protocol)
    d. NIC (network interface card)

_____ 9. Which type of home network uses radio waves, instead of cables, to transmit data?
    a. powerline
    b. phoneline
    c. Ethernet
    d. HomeRF

_____ 10. What is used by applications such as air navigation, television and radio broadcast, video conferencing, paging, and global positioning systems?
    a. coaxial cable
    b. communications satellites
    c. infrared
    d. microwaves

Fill in the Blanks

1. A(n) _____ provides for storage and management of a company's document.

2. A voice mail system usually provides an individual _____ for each user, which can be accessed to listen to messages.

3. A(n) _____ is a network that covers a large geographic area using a communications channel that combines many types of media, such as telephone lines, cables, and radio waves.

4. A(n) _____ is a dedicated server that stores and provides access to a database.

5. A(n) _____ is a dedicated server that stores and manages files.

6. On a(n) _____ network, a cable forms a closed loop with all computers and devices arranged along the loop.

7. The _____, or 802.16, standard provides wireless broadband Internet access at a reasonable cost over long distances to business and home users.

8. A(n) _____ line is a type of always-on connection that is established between two communications devices (unlike a dial-up line where the connection is reestablished each time it is used).

9. A(n) _____ line is any of several types of long-distance digital telephone lines that carry multiple signals over a single communications line.

10. _____ is the time it takes a signal to travel from one location to another on a network.

Complete the Table

SPEEDS OF VARIOUS INTERNET CONNECTIONS

Type of Line	Approximate Monthly Cost	Transfer Rates
_____	Local or long-distance rates	Up to 56 Kbps
ISDN	$10 to $40	_____
DSL	_____	128 Kbps to 8.45 Mbps
Cable TV (CATV)	_____	128 Kbps to 36 Mbps
_____	$35 to $70	256 Kbps to 10 Mbps
_____	$200 to $700	128 Kbps to 768 Kbps
_____	$500 to $1,000	1.544 Mbps
T3	$5,000 to $15,000	_____
_____	_____	155 Mbps to 622 Mbps, can reach 10 Gbps

Things to Think About

1. What uses of communications technologies have had the greatest impact on personal interactions? What uses have had the greatest impact on business interactions? Why?

2. What network capability — hardware sharing, data and information sharing, software sharing, or facilitated communications — would be most important to a school? To a business? To a government office? Why?

3. What network topology — bus, ring, or star — would be best for a school? For a business? For a government office? Why?

4. What might be the advantages of connecting multiple computers in your home in a home network? Which type of home network would you use? Why?

Puzzle

All of the words described below appear in the puzzle. Words may be either forward or backward, across, up and down, or diagonal. Circle each word as you find it.

```
Z C A Y U E T S M C H G Z O E I K G W C Z A P J O G S
X M D H U M V I X B W K X P E J T M W O F T W F U F N
C E I L A N N K D N A B D A O R B M H A Z D C I M W L
U P N Z W I M M Z G S O K I H J N B N X D E W E O S H
W E D I I O E N E Z W K K G Z W A R J I S Y R E D O T
A S L D L D E U E D G I L T O Q Y V E A V A E A S R D
S D G X O E F N Z T J L P E E A O X P L W I Z T D Y I
U P S M W K N V I R W Q T E F I D S A P M Z N Y P Q W
X E U S I A N O V L Y O P Y C T T G U D U E J E V M D
F Z B B H R B Z H S 1 B R E E N S O S I I N S C Z Y N
Z J Y C N I T A Q P G T M K S Q R R B L J G P S A A A
M X G L O W R E S N Z A H J N G K L C I S Y K K U X B
X P N J H L S Z P E I N M Q E V M R F E Q E N X Y O M
E E I J W I L M J L B E J F C C S A H N D E I T K A Y
E B V F O C P A O A E A X E I O I Y N H K D L Q N S C
Y X I N O P A M B N Z T N F L X U R U R X I N M I A I
H G E Z N K X R N O W W M D K F O E S U D X W U L P T
V I C M M E T J T L R D D Q R T E T A J I G O L P E P
R V E O X S M X A O X A Y K O O O U G G A D D T U G O
V Y R O R B T L S I P K T A W K V O Q G L O C I E I R
X Q E O P U K D E W K S R E T E I R T Z U P T P T L E
D R U U G H F F R U J T T I E N P N K T P F P L A C B
Q M I C R O W A V E S L Q O N X X C S T A R U E L X I
S C S T O U C M E T G Y X L H G X F Q H F S V X U H F
M F A S W E T S R V A N A L O G O N N P M W R I D C Q
S K Z G I W R E E P O T R E E P S P S D P A V N O X A
B T S O Z O B R R E V T N A R O P P K G R L E G M A K
```

Type of signal that consists of a continuous electrical wave

Allows callers to leave a voice message for the called party

Work together with others connected to a server

Application that helps people work together on projects over a network

Collection of computers and devices connected by communications channels

Legal agreement that allows multiple users to run a software package simultaneously

Network that connects computers in a limited geographical area

Computers on a client/server LAN that rely on the server for resources

Controls access to the hardware and software on a client/server LAN

High-speed network that connects LANs in a city or town

Type of network that consists of a single cable to which all computers connect

Type of network with all computers arranged along a closed loop

Type of network in which all devices connect to a central computer

Worldwide telephone network that handles voice-oriented telephone calls

Temporary connection that uses one or more analog telephone lines

Technique that allows a telephone line to carry three or more signals at once

Type of DSL that supports faster transfer rates when receiving data

Communications device that converts between digital and analog signals

To change a digital signal into an analog signal

Device that provides a central point for cables in a network

Type of media that can transmit only one signal at a time

Type of media that can transmit multiple signals simultaneously

Electrical disturbance that can degrade communications

Radio waves that provide a high-speed signal transmission

Transmission from an earth-based station to a communications satellite

Transmission from a communications satellite to an earth-based station

Device that accepts the transmission of data, instructions, or information

Line that is a type of always-on connection

An area with the capability of wireless Internet connectivity

A navigation system that consists of one or more earth-based receivers that accept and analyze signals sent by satellites in order to determine the receiver's geographic location

A means for smart phone users, for example, to send and receive brief text messages on their devices

Standard that defines how data transmits across telephone lines or other means

Allows users connected to a network to transfer money from one bank account to another via telephone lines or other media

A network covering a large geographic area

A simple, inexpensive network that typically connects fewer than 10 computers

A special series of bits that function like a ticket

The most popular T-carrier line

A communications device that connects multiple computers and transmits data to the correct destination on a network

Network that uses existing telephone lines in the home

The amount of data, instructions, and information that can travel over a communications channel

Cable consisting of a single copper wire surrounded by at least three layers

Cable consisting of dozens or hundreds of thin strands of glass or plastic

Self Test Answers

Matching	True/False	Multiple Choice	Fill in the Blanks
1. *i* [p. 463]	1. *F* [p. 460]	1. *d* [p. 471]	1. *document management system* [p. 468]
2. *h* [p. 464]	2. *T* [p. 471]	2. *c* [p. 473]	2. *voice mailbox* [p. 468]
3. *a* [p. 464]	3. *T* [p. 471]	3. *c* [p. 474]	3. *wide area network* or *WAN* [p. 472]
4. *b* [p. 465]	4. *F* [p. 473]	4. *a* [p. 476]	4. *database server* [p. 473]
5. *f* [p. 466]	5. *T* [p. 474]	5. *a* [p. 477]	5. *file server* [p. 473]
6. *c* [p. 467]	6. *T* [p. 477]	6. *c* [p. 482]	6. *ring* [p. 474]
7. *k* [p. 468]	7. *F* [p. 478]	7. *b* [p. 485]	7. *WiMAX* [p. 479]
8. *j* [p. 468]	8. *F* [p. 484]	8. *d* [p. 486]	8. *dedicated* [p. 482]
9. *g* [p. 468]	9. *F* [p. 489]	9. *d* [p. 490]	9. *T-carrier* [p. 483]
10. *l* [p. 468]	10. *F* [p. 493]	10. *b* [p. 496]	10. *Latency* [p. 491]

Complete the Table

SPEEDS OF VARIOUS INTERNET CONNECTIONS

Type of Line	Approximate Monthly Cost	Transfer Rates
Dial-up	Local or long-distance rates	Up to 56 Kbps
ISDN	$10 to $40	*Up to 128 Kbps*
DSL	*$15 to $40*	128 Kbps to 8.45 Mbps
Cable TV (CATV)	*$20 to $45*	128 Kbps to 36 Mbps
Fixed Wireless	$35 to $70	256 Kbps to 10 Mbps
Fractional T1	$200 to $700	128 Kbps to 768 Kbps
T1	$500 to $1,000	1.544 Mbps
T3	$5,000 to $15,000	*44.736 Mbps*
ATM	*$3,000 or more*	155 Mbps to 622 Mbps, can reach 10 Gbps

Things to Think About

Answers will vary.

Puzzle Answer

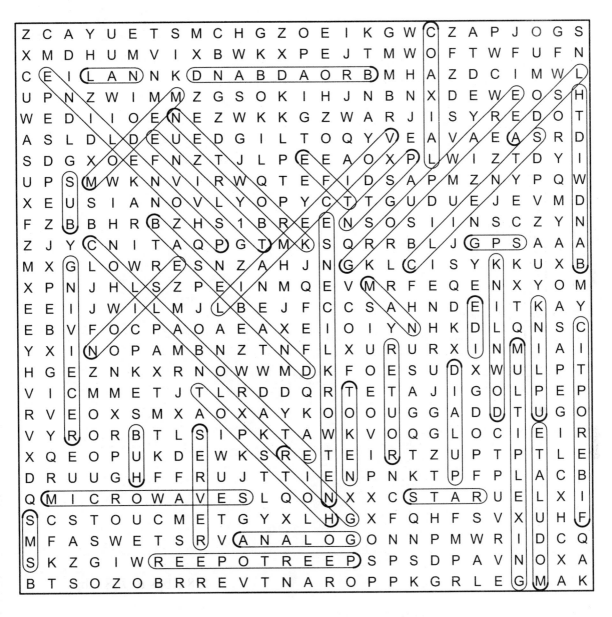

Notes

DISCOVERING COMPUTERS 2007

STUDY GUIDE

CHAPTER 10

Database Management

Chapter Overview

This chapter discusses how data and information are valuable assets to an organization. The chapter also presents methods for maintaining high-quality data and assessing the quality of valuable information. It then discusses the advantages of organizing data in a database and describes various types of databases. It also presents the roles of the database analysts and administrators.

Chapter Objectives

After completing this chapter, you should be able to:

- Define the term *database*
- Identify the qualities of valuable information
- Explain why data is important to an organization
- Discuss the terms *character, field, record,* and *file*
- Identify file maintenance techniques
- Differentiate between a file processing system approach and the database approach

- Discuss the functions common to most DBMSs
- Describe characteristics of relational, object-oriented, and multidimensional databases
- Explain how to interact with Web databases
- Discuss the responsibilities of database analysts and administrators

Chapter Outline

I. Databases, data, and information [p. 514]

A database is _____

_____

- Data is _____
- Information is _____

Computers process data in a database into information.

Database software, or a database management system (DBMS), is _____

_____

A. Data integrity [p. 516]

Data integrity is_____

Garbage in, garbage out (GIGO) is a computer phrase that means _____

_____

B. Qualities of valuable information [p. 516]

Valuable information is accurate, verifiable, timely, organized, accessible, useful, and cost-effective.

- Accurate information is _____
- Verifiable information can _____
- Timely information has_____
- Organized information is_____
- Accessible information is _____
- Useful information has _____
- Cost-effective information should _____

II. The hierarchy of data [p. 517]

Data is organized in a hierarchy in which each higher level consists of one or more elements from the lower level preceding it.

A. Characters [p. 518]

A character — such as a number, letter, punctuation mark, or other symbol — is represented by a byte (8 bits grouped together in a unit).

B. Fields [p. 518]

A field is _____

A field name uniquely identifies each field.

Characteristics such as data type and field size define each field.

The field size defines _____

The data type specifies _____

Common data types include:

- _____   - _____   - _____
- _____   - _____   - _____
- _____   - _____   - _____

C. Records [p. 519]

A record is _____

A key field (or primary key) is _____

D. Files [p. 519]

A data file is _____

_____

A database includes a group of related data files.

III. Maintaining data [p. 520]

File maintenance refers to _____

A. Adding records [p. 520]

Users add new records when _____

B. Changing records [p. 521]

Generally, you change records for two reasons:

(1) _____

(2) _____

C. Deleting records [p. 522]

Users delete records from a file when _____

D. Validating data [p. 522]

Validation is _____

A validity check analyzes _____

Validation rules reduce _____

Types of validity checks include alphabetic, numeric, range, consistency, and completeness.

1. Alphabetic/numeric check [p. 523]

An alphabetic check ensures _____

_____

A numeric check ensures _____

2. Range check [p. 523]

A range check determines _____

_____

3. Consistency check [p. 523]

A consistency check tests _____

_____

4. Completeness check [p. 523]

A completeness check verifies _____

_____

5. Check digit [p. 523]

A check digit confirms _____

_____

IV. File processing versus databases [p. 524]

A. File processing systems [p. 524]

In a typical file processing system, each department has _____

_____

_____

Disadvantages of file processing systems:

- Data redundancy — _____

_____

- Isolated data — _____

_____

B. The database approach [p. 524]

With the database approach, many programs and users can _____

_____

Users can access the data in a database using database software, also called a database management system (DBMS). Instead of working with a DBMS, some users interact with a front end.

A front end is _____

The back end is _____

Advantages of the database approach:

- Reduced data redundancy — _____

_____

- Improved data integrity — _____

_____

- Shared data — _____

_____

- Easier access — _____

_____

- Reduced development time — _____

_____

Disadvantages of the database approach: _____

_____

V. Database management systems [p. 526]

A database management system (DBMS) is _____

_____

Common elements of a DBMS:

A. Data dictionary [p. 527]

A data dictionary (or repository) contains _____

_____

Metadata is _____

_____

A DBMS uses the data dictionary to perform validation checks and maintain
the integrity of data. The data dictionary allows a default value to be specified.
A default value is _____

B. File retrieval and maintenance [p. 528]

A query is _____

_____

A DBMS offers several methods to access its data.

1. Query language [p. 528]

A query language consists of _____

_____

2. Query by example [p. 528]

Query by example (QBE) is used to _____

_____

3. Form [p. 530]

A form, sometimes called a data entry form, is _____

_____

An e-form (short for electronic form) typically is_____

_____

4. Report generator [p. 530]

A report generator (or report writer) allows _____

_____

C. Data security [p. 530]

Access privileges define _____

_____

- With read-only privileges, you can _____

  _____

- With full-update privileges, you can _____

  _____

D. Backup and recovery [p. 531]

   A DBMS provides a variety of techniques to restore a database:

   - A backup is _____

   - A log is _____

     The before image is _____

     The after image is _____

   - A DBMS often provides a recovery utility to restore a database.

     In a rollforward (or forward recovery), the DBMS uses _____

     _____

     In a rollback (or backward recovery), the DBMS uses _____

     _____

     Continuous backup is _____

     _____

VI. Relational, object-oriented, and multidimensional databases [p. 532]

    A data model consists of _____

    _____

    Three popular data models are relational, object-oriented, and multidimensional.
    Object-relational databases combine _____

    _____

A. Relational databases [p. 533]

   A relational database stores _____

   _____

   A developer of a relational database refers to a file as a relation, a record as a
   tuple, and a field as an attribute. A user of a relational database, by contrast,
   refers to _____

   _____

Data Terminology		
File Processing Environment	Relational Database Developer	Relational Database User
File	_____	_____
Record	_____	_____
Field	_____	_____

A relationship is _____

_____

Normalization is _____

_____

1. SQL [p. 534]

   Structured Query Language (SQL) is _____

   _____

B. Object-oriented databases [p. 534]

   An object-oriented database (OODB) stores _____

   An object is _____

   _____

   Advantages of an object-oriented database relative to relational databases:

   _____

   _____

   _____

   Applications appropriate for an object-oriented database:

   • A multimedia database stores _____

   • A groupware database stores _____

   • A computer-aided design (CAD) database stores _____

   _____

   • A hypertext database contains _____

     A hypermedia database contains _____

   • A Web database links _____

   1. Object query language [p. 535]

      An object query language (OQL) is _____

      _____

C. Multidimensional databases [p. 535]

   A multidimensional database stores _____

A hypercube is _____

_____

The key advantage of the multidimensional database is _____

_____

1. Data warehouses [p. 536]
   A data warehouse is _____

   _____

   A distributed database is _____

   _____

   Data mining is _____

   _____

   A data mart contains _____

   _____

VII. Web databases [p. 536]

   Much of the information on the Web exists in databases. Users access and provide information to Web databases by entering data into a form on a Web page, the front end to the database.

   A database server is _____

   _____

   A CGI (Common Gateway Interface) script manages _____

   _____

VIII. Database administration [p. 537]

   The role of coordinating the use of a database belongs to the database analysts and administrators, who need cooperation from all database users.

   A. Database design guidelines [p. 537]

      These guidelines make it easier for a user to query a database:

      1. Determine _____

      2. Design _____

         _____

      3. Design _____

         _____

         _____

      4. Determine _____

B. Role of the database analysts and administrators [p. 538]

The database analyst (DA), or data modeler, focuses on _____

_____

The database administrator (DBA) creates _____

_____

C. Role of the employee as a user [p. 538]

The user's responsibilities are _____

_____

Self Test

Matching

1.	___	accurate	a.	a data type that holds lengthy text entries
2.	___	verifiable	b.	type of information that can be proven correct or incorrect
3.	___	timely		
4.	___	organized	c.	also known as the BLOB data type
5.	___	accessible	d.	information that is arranged to suit the needs and requirements of the decision maker
6.	___	useful		
7.	___	Text	e.	type of information that has meaning to the person who receives it
8.	___	Yes/No	f.	data type that can include only numbers
9.	___	Memo	g.	also known as the alphanumeric data type
10.	___	Object	h.	type of information that is available when the decision maker needs it

i. type of information that is error-free

j. also known as the Boolean data type

k. type of information with an age suited to its use

l. type of information that should give more value than it costs to produce

True/False

___ 1. Correct data guarantees that information is correct.

___ 2. In the hierarchy of data, a field contains records, a record contains files, and a file contains databases.

___ 3. A data type uniquely identifies each field in a database.

___ 4. Deleting unneeded records reduces the size of files and creates additional storage space.

___ 5. Two of the advantages of file processing systems are no data redundancy and shared data.

___ 6. Database management systems are available for many sizes and types of computers.

___ 7. Like a form, you use report generators to retrieve and maintain data.

___ 8. In a rollback, or backward recovery, the DBMS uses the log to reenter changes made to the database since the last database save or backup.

_____ 9. A database typically is based on multiple data models.

_____ 10. Hypermedia databases contain text, graphics, video, and sound.

Multiple Choice

_____ 1. What is a collection of unprocessed items?
    a. information
    b. data
    c. text
    d. tuple

_____ 2. In the ASCII and EBCDIC coding schemes, each byte represents a single what?
    a. field
    b. record
    c. character
    d. file

_____ 3. What is the smallest unit of data that you can access?
    a. character
    b. field
    c. record
    d. file

_____ 4. What does a completeness check do?
    a. ensures that only the correct type of data is entered into a field
    b. tests data in multiple fields to determine if a relationship is reasonable
    c. determines whether a number is within a specified range
    d. verifies a required field contains data

_____ 5. Which of the following is *not* an advantage of the database approach?
    a. reduced data redundancy
    b. decreased vulnerability
    c. improved data integrity
    d. easier reporting

_____ 6. A report generator, or report writer, is used only for what purpose?
    a. enter data
    b. change data
    c. retrieve data
    d. maintain data

_____ 7. Access, Informix, and SQL Server are popular DBMSs based on what data model?
    a. relational databases
    b. object-oriented databases
    c. object-relational databases
    d. multidimensional databases

_____ 8. How does a relational database developer refer to a record?
   a. table
   b. relation
   c. tuple
   d. attribute

_____ 9. A user of a relational database refers to a record as what?
   a. row
   b. column
   c. table
   d. tuple

_____ 10. The multiple dimensions in a multidimensional database sometimes are known as what?
   a. hypertext
   b. OQL
   c. data model
   d. hypercube

Fill in the Blanks

1. A(n) _____ includes a collection of data organized so you can access, retrieve, and use the data.

2. Data _____ identifies the quality of the data in a database.

3. _____ is a computer phrase that means you cannot create correct information from data that is incorrect.

4. A(n) _____ is software that allows you to create, access, and manage a database.

5. Some call the data dictionary _____ because it contains details about data.

6. A(n) _____ is a window on the screen that provides areas for entering or changing data in a database.

7. In addition to data, a relational database stores data _____, which are connections within the data.

8. A relational database is a two-dimensional table, but a(n) _____ can store more than two dimensions of data.

9. The _____, or data modeler, focuses on the meaning and usage of data in deciding the proper placement of fields, defines the relationships among data, and identifies users' access privileges.

10. The _____ creates and maintains the data dictionary, manages security of the database, and checks backup and recovery procedures.

Complete the Table

POPULAR DATABASE MANAGEMENT SYSTEMS

Database	Manufacturer	Computer Type
Access	_____	Personal computer, server, mobile devices
Adabas	Software AG	_____
_____	IBM Corporation	Personal computer, server, mainframe
GemFire	_____	Server
Ingres	Computer Associates International, Inc.	_____
_____	Oracle Corporation	Personal computer, server, mainframe, mobile devices
SQL Server	Microsoft Corporation	_____
_____	Microsoft Corporation	Personal computer, server

Things to Think About

1. Why are deleted records sometimes *flagged* so they are not processed, instead of being removed immediately?

2. What type of validity check — alphabetic/numeric, range, consistency, completeness, or check digit — would be most useful when reviewing your answers on an exam? Why?

3. What characteristics of valuable information are most important? On what, if any, factors might your answer depend? Why?

4. Is it a crime to access confidential information in a database without authorization? Why or why not? Does it depend on the information accessed?

Puzzle

Use the given clues to complete the crossword puzzle.

Across

3. Validity check that tests if data in associated fields is logical
4. Information arranged to suit the needs and requirements of the decision maker
6. Data that is organized, meaningful, and useful
11. Type of database that stores images, audio clips, and/or video clips
12. Links to an e-form on a Web page
13. Collection of related records stored on a disk
15. Collection of raw, unprocessed facts, figures, and symbols
17. Request for specific data from a database
20. Information that gives more value that it costs to produce
23. On-screen window that provides areas for entering or changing data
24. Utility that uses the logs/backups to restore a database that is damaged or destroyed
27. Database that stores data in objects
29. Phrase that means that you cannot create correct information from data that is incorrect
30. Information that is available when the decision maker needs it
32. Type of database that exists in many separate locations throughout a network
33. Uniquely identifies each record in a file
34. Combination of one or more characters

Down

1. Validity check that verifies a required field contains data
2. Refers to the procedures that keep data current
5. Software that allows a database to be created, accessed, or managed
7. Process designed to ensure data contains the least amount of duplication
8. Specifies the kind of data a field can contain
9. Consists of rules and standards that define how data is organized
10. Type of value that the DBMS initially displays in a field
14. Query language often used with object-relational databases
16. Type of information that is error-free
18. Group of related fields
19. Copy of a record prior to a charge
21. Information that can be proven correct or incorrect
22. A number(s) or character(s) appended to or inserted into a primary key value
25. Validity check that determines whether a number is within specified limits
26. Information with meaning to the person who receives it
28. A copy of the entire database made on a regular basis
31. Information with an age suited to its use

Self Test Answers

Matching	True/False	Multiple Choice	Fill in the Blanks
1. *i* [p. 516]	1. *F* [p. 516]	1. *b* [p. 514]	1. *database* [p. 514]
2. *b* [p. 516]	2. *F* [p. 517]	2. *c* [p. 518]	2. *integrity* [p. 516]
3. *k* [p. 516]	3. *F* [p. 518]	3. *b* [p. 518]	3. *Garbage in garbage out* or *GIGO* [p. 516]
4. *d* [p. 516]	4. *T* [p. 522]	4. *d* [p. 523]	
5. *h* [p. 516]	5. *F* [p. 524]	5. *b* [p. 525]	4. *database management system (DBMS)* [p. 526]
6. *e* [p. 517]	6. *T* [p. 526]	6. *c* [p. 533]	
7. *g* [p. 518]	7. *F* [p. 530]	7. *a* [p. 532]	5. *metadata* [p. 527]
8. *j* [p. 518]	8. *F* [p. 532]	8. *c* [p. 533]	6. *form* or *data entry form* [p. 530]
9. *a* [p. 518]	9. *F* [p. 532]	9. *a* [p. 533]	7. *relationships* [p. 533]
10. *c* [p. 518]	10. *T* [p. 534]	10. *d* [p. 535]	8. *multidimensional database* [p. 535]
			9. *database analyst* or *DA* [p. 538]
			10. *database administrator* or *DBA* [p. 538]

Complete the Table

POPULAR DATABASE MANAGEMENT SYSTEMS

Database	Manufacturer	Computer Type
Access	*Microsoft Corporation*	Personal computer, server, mobile devices
Adabas	Software AG	*Server, mainframe*
DB2	IBM Corporation	Personal computer, server, mainframe
GemFire	*GemStone Systems, Inc.*	Server
Ingres	Computer Associates International, Inc.	*Personal computer, server, mainframe*

Database	Manufacturer	Computer Type
Oracle Database	Oracle Corporation	Personal computer, server, mainframe, mobile devices
SQL Server	Microsoft Corporation	*Server, personal computer, PDA*
Visual FoxPro	Microsoft Corporation	Personal computer, server

Things to Think About

Answers will vary.

Puzzle Answer

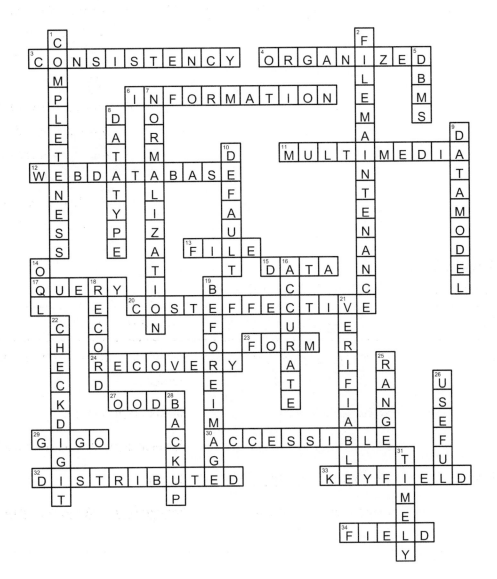

Notes

DISCOVERING COMPUTERS 2007

STUDY GUIDE

CHAPTER 11

Computer Security, Ethics, and Privacy

Chapter Overview

This chapter identifies some potential computer risks and the safeguards that schools, businesses, and individuals can implement to minimize these risks. Wireless security risks and safeguards also are discussed. The chapter presents ethical issues surrounding information accuracy, intellectual property rights, codes of conduct, and information privacy. The chapter ends with a discussion of computer-related health issues, their preventions, and ways to keep the environment healthy.

Chapter Objectives

After completing this chapter, you should be able to:

- Describe the types of computer security risks
- Identify ways to safeguard against computer viruses, worms, Trojan horses, denial of service attacks, back doors, and spoofing
- Discuss techniques to prevent unauthorized computer access and use
- Identify safeguards against hardware theft and vandalism
- Explain the ways software manufacturers protect against software piracy
- Define encryption and explain why it is necessary

- Discuss the types of devices available that protect from system failure
- Explain the options available for backing up computer resources
- Identify risks and safeguards associated with wireless connections
- Recognize issues related to information accuracy, rights, and conduct
- Discuss issues surrounding information privacy
- Discuss ways to prevent health-related disorders and injuries due to computer use

Chapter Outline

I. Computer security risks [p. 556]

A computer security risk is _____

_____

A computer crime is _____

_____

Cybercrime refers to _____

A hacker is _____

A cracker is _____

A script kiddie is _____

A cyberextortionist _____

A cyberterrorist is _____

II. Internet and network attacks [p. 558]
An online security service is _____

The Computer Emergency Response Team Coordination Center (CERT/CC) is __
_____

A. Computer viruses, worms, and Trojan horses [p. 558]
   ● A computer virus is _____

   ● A worm is _____

   ● A Trojan horse is _____

   Malware (short for malicious software) is _____

   The payload is _____

   Viruses are activated in four basic ways:
   (1) _____
   (2) _____
   (3) _____
   (4) _____

B. Safeguards against computer viruses, worms, and Trojan horses [p. 560]

A trusted source is _____

_____

A macro is _____

_____

An antivirus program protects _____

_____

Antivirus programs can detect viruses by looking for virus signatures or by inoculating existing program files.

- A virus signature (or virus definition) is _____

_____

- To inoculate a program file, the antivirus program records _____

_____

If a virus cannot be removed, the infected file can be quarantined or, for boot sector viruses, the computer can be restarted with a recovery disk.

- A quarantine is _____

_____

A virus hoax is _____

_____

C. Denial of service attacks [p. 562]

A denial of service attack (DoS attack) _____

_____

A DDoS (distributed DoS) attack is _____

_____

A zombie is _____

_____

D. Back doors [p. 562]

A back door is _____

_____

E. Spoofing [p. 563]

Spoofing is _____

_____

F. Safeguards against DoS attacks, back doors, and IP spoofing [p. 563]

To defend against these attacks, users can implement firewall solutions, install intrusion detection software, and set up honeypots.

G. Firewalls [p. 563]

A firewall is _____

_____

A proxy server is _____

_____

A personal firewall utility is _____

_____

H. Intrusion detection software [p. 564]

Intrusion detection software analyzes _____

_____

I. Honeypots [p. 564]

A honeypot is _____

_____

III. Unauthorized access and use [p. 564]

Unauthorized access is _____

_____

Unauthorized use is _____

_____

A. Safeguards against unauthorized access and use [p. 565]

An acceptable use policy (AUP) outlines _____

_____

B. Identifying and authenticating users [p. 565]

An access control is _____

_____

An audit trail is _____

_____

Access controls often are implemented using a two-phase process:

• Identification verifies _____

_____

• Authentication verifies _____

_____

1. User names and passwords [p. 566]

A user name, or user ID, is _____

_____

A password is _____

_____

2. Possessed objects [p. 567]

A possessed object is _____

_____

A personal identification number (PIN) is _____

_____

3. Biometric devices [p. 567]

A biometric device authenticates _____

_____

IV. Hardware theft and vandalism [p. 569]

Hardware theft is_____

_____

Hardware vandalism is _____

_____

A. Safeguards against hardware theft and vandalism [p. 569]

To reduce the chances of hardware theft, companies, schools, and individuals

can _____

_____

_____

_____

V. Software theft [p. 570]

Software theft occurs when _____

_____

_____

Software piracy is _____

_____

A. Safeguards against software theft [p. 570]

A license agreement is _____

_____

A single-user license agreement, also called an end-user license agreement
(EULA), permits users to:

*   _____

*   _____

*   _____

A single-user license agreement does *not* permit users to:

*   _____

*   _____

- _____
- _____

The Business Software Alliance (BSA) operates _____

_____

During the product activation, users provide _____

_____

VI. Information theft [p. 571]
Information theft occurs when _____

_____

   A. Safeguards against information theft [p. 572]
   B. Encryption [p. 572]
     Encryption is _____

_____

     To decrypt data means _____

_____

- Plaintext is _____
- Ciphertext is _____
- An encryption key is _____

_____

     Pretty Good Privacy (PGP) is _____

_____

     A digital signature is _____

_____

     A hash is _____

_____

     Some browsers offer 40-bit encryption. Many also offer _____

_____

     A secure site is _____

_____

    1. Digital certificates [p. 573]
       A digital certificate is _____

_____

       A certificate authority (CA) is _____

_____

2. Secure Sockets Layer [p. 574]
    Secure Sockets Layer (SSL) provides _____

    _____

3. Secure HTTP [p. 574]
    Secure HTTP (S-HTTP) allows _____

    _____

    A virtual private network (VPN) provides _____

    _____

VII. System failure [p. 574]
    A system failure is _____

    _____

Electrical disturbances:

*   Noise is _____

    _____

*   An undervoltage occurs _____

    _____

    A brownout is _____

    _____

    A blackout is _____

    _____

*   An overvoltage, or power surge, occurs _____

    _____

    A spike occurs_____

A. Safeguards against system failure [p. 574]
    A surge protector (or surge suppressor) uses _____

    _____

    Surge protectors should meet specifications of the Underwriters Laboratories
    (UL) 1449 standard and have a Joule (the unit of energy that can be absorbed
    before damage occurs) rating of at least 200.
    An uninterruptible power supply (UPS) is _____

    _____

*   A standby UPS (or offline UPS) switches _____

    _____

*   An online UPS always runs _____
    A fault-tolerant computer has _____

    _____

VIII.   Backing up – the ultimate safeguard [p. 576]
        A backup is _____
        _____

        To back up a file, you make _____
        _____

        To restore a file, you copy _____
        _____

        Offsite means _____
        _____

        Types of backup:
        •   A full backup copies _____
            _____

        •   A selective backup copies _____
            _____

        A three-generation backup policy preserves_____
        _____

        •   The grandparent is _____
            _____

        •   The parent is _____
            _____

        •   The child is _____
            _____

        An online backup service is _____
        _____

IX.   Wireless security [p. 576]
        War driving is _____
        _____

        War flying is _____
        _____

        •   Wired Equivalent Privacy (WEP) is _____
            _____

        •   Wi-Fi Protected Access (WPA) is _____
            _____

        •   An 802.11i network conforms to _____
            _____

X. Ethics and society [p. 578]

Computer ethics are _____

_____

A. Information accuracy [p. 579]

Many people access information maintained by other people or companies, such as on the Internet. You should evaluate the value of a Web page before relying on its content. Concerns also arise about the ethics of using computers to alter output, such as retouching photographs.

B. Intellectual property rights [p. 579]

Intellectual property (IP) refers to _____

_____

Intellectual property rights are _____

_____

A copyright gives _____

_____

Digital rights management is _____

_____

C. Codes of conduct [p. 580]

An IT (information technology) code of conduct is _____

_____

_____

XI. Information privacy [p. 580]

Information privacy refers to _____

_____

Companies and employers use several techniques to collect personal data.

A. Electronic profiles [p. 581]

Electronic profiles can include very personal data. National marketing firms and Internet advertising firms create electronic profiles of individuals by combining merchant databases with information from public sources.

B. Cookies [p. 582]

A cookie is _____

_____

Web sites use cookies for a variety of purposes:

- _____

- _____

- _____

    A session cookie is _____

- _____

- _____

C. Spyware and adware [p. 583]

Spyware is_____

_____

- Adware is _____

- A Web bug is _____

D. Spam [p. 584]

Spam is _____

_____

Spim is _____

Spit is _____

- E-mail filtering is _____

- An anti-spam program attempts _____

E. Phishing [p. 584]

Phishing is_____

_____

Pharming is _____

_____

F. Privacy laws [p. 585]

Common points in federal and state laws regarding the storage and disclosure of personal data:

1. _____

2. _____

3. _____

4. _____

Federal laws dealing specifically with computers:

- The loophole in the Fair Credit Reporting Act is that _____

_____

G. Social engineering [p. 586]

Social engineering is _____

_____

H. Employee monitoring [p. 586]

Employee monitoring involves _____

_____

I. Content filtering [p. 586]

Content filtering is _____

_____

The Internet Content Rating Association (ICRA) is _____

_____

Web filtering software is _____

_____

J. Computer forensics [p. 587]

Computer forensics (or digital forensics, network forensics, or cyberforensics)

is _____

_____

XII. Health concerns of computer use [p. 587]

The widespread use of computers has led to some important health concerns.

A. Computers and health risks [p. 587]

A repetitive stress injury (RSI) is _____

_____

Computer-related RSIs include tendonitis and carpal tunnel syndrome.

- Tendonitis is _____

_____

- Carpal tunnel syndrome (CTS) is _____

_____

Another health-related condition due to computer usage is computer vision

syndrome (CVS). You may have CVS if you have: _____

_____

B. Ergonomics and workplace design [p. 589]

Ergonomics is _____

_____

_____

C. Computer addiction [p. 589]

Computer addiction occurs when _____

_____

Symptoms of computer addiction:

- _____
- _____
- _____

- _____
- _____
- _____

D. Green computing [p. 590]

Green computing involves _____

_____

Self Test

Matching

1. _____ virus

2. _____ worm

3. _____ Trojan horse

4. _____ payload

5. _____ DoS

6. _____ PIN

7. _____ biometric device

8. _____ SSL

9. _____ UPS

10. _____ RSI

a. type of attack whose purpose is to disrupt access to the Web

b. injury of the muscles, nerves, tendons, ligaments, and joints

c. converts readable data into unreadable characters to prevent unauthorized access

d. translates a personal characteristic into a digital code for comparison with a digital code verifying a physical or behavioral characteristic

e. a potentially damaging program that infects a computer and negatively affects the way the computer works without the user's knowledge or permission

f. standard that defines acceptable levels of radiation from monitors

g. hides within or looks like a legitimate program

h. numeric password assigned by a company or selected by a user

i. provides encryption of all data that passes between a client and an Internet server

j. copies itself repeatedly in memory or on a disk drive until no memory or disk space remains

k. destructive event a virus is intended to deliver

l. contains surge protection circuits and one or more batteries that can provide power during a power loss

True/False

_____ 1. Any illegal act involving a computer generally is referred to as a cybercrime.

_____ 2. Typically, you have to reformat a hard disk to remove a virus.

_____ 3. All networked and online computer users should have a firewall.

_____ 4. An audit trail is a program designed to entice an intruder to hack into the computer.

_____ 5. Hardware theft and vandalism pose a significant threat to all computer users.

_____ 6. Information transmitted over networks offers a high degree of risk because unscrupulous users can intercept it during transmission.

_____ 7. Copyright law gives the public fair use to copyrighted material.

_____ 8. In a pharming scam, a perpetrator attempts to obtain your personal and financial information, except they do so via spoofing.

_____ 9. The widespread use of computers has led to some important health concerns.

_____ 10. PCs, display devices, and printers should comply with ENERGY STAR program guidelines.

Multiple Choice

_____ 1. Which of the following is an instruction saved in an application, such as a spreadsheet program, in which viruses sometimes are hidden?
   a. script
   b. link
   c. toolset
   d. macro

_____ 2. Which of the following is a known specific pattern of virus code?
   a. virus inoculation
   b. virus password
   c. virus signature
   d. virus glossary

_____ 3. Which of the following records both successful and unsuccessful access attempts?
   a. virus signature
   b. virus definition
   c. audit trail
   d. all of the above

_____ 4. Which of the following verifies that an individual is the person he or she claims to be?
   a. identification
   b. authentication
   c. detection
   d. backup

_____ 5. What is encrypted data called?
   a. plaintext
   b. keytext
   c. cryptext
   d. ciphertext

_____ 6. Which of the following types of certificates is a notice that guarantees the legitimacy of a user or a Web site?
   a. UPS
   b. digital certificate
   c. DoS
   d. CERT/CC

_____ 7. In which of the following types of backup do users choose which folders and files to include in a backup?
   a. selective backup
   b. partial backup
   c. full backup
   d. incremental backup

_____ 8. Which of the following is a small text file that a Web server stores on your computer?
   a. cookie
   b. audit trail
   c. worm
   d. Trojan horse

_____ 9. Which of the following is used to monitor online habits of Web site visitors?
   a. filter
   b. spam
   c. Web bug
   d. cookie

_____ 10. What law makes it illegal to circumvent antipiracy schemes in commercial software?
   a. Electronic Communications Privacy Act
   b. Digital Millennium Copyright Act
   c. Computer Matching and Privacy Protection Act
   d. Computer Fraud and Abuse Act

Fill in the Blanks

1. A(n) _____ is someone who uses the Internet or network to destroy or damage computers for political reasons.

2. A(n) _____ source is a company or person you believe will *not* send a virus-infected file knowingly.

3. To _____ a program file, the antivirus program records information such as the file size and file creation date, and then uses this information to detect if a virus tampers with the data describing the program file.

4. Unauthorized _____ is the use of a computer or network without permission.

5. A(n) _____ is a private combination of characters associated with the user name that allows access to certain computer resources.

6. Software _____ is the unauthorized and illegal duplication of copyrighted software.

7. _____ is the process of converting readable data into unreadable characters to prevent unauthorized access.

8. A(n) _____ is a duplicate of a file, program, or disk that can be used if the original is lost, damaged, or destroyed.

9. In _____, perpetrators attempt to connect to wireless networks via their notebook computer while driving a vehicle through areas they suspect of having a wireless network.

10. Computer _____ are the moral guidelines that govern the use of computers and information systems.

Complete the Table

MAJOR U.S. GOVERNMENT LAWS CONCERNING PRIVACY

DATE	LAW	PURPOSE
2003	_____ _____	Gives law enforcement the right to impose penalties on people using the Internet to distribute spam.
2002	_____ _____	Requires corporate officers, auditors, and attorneys of publicly traded companies to follow strict financial reporting guidelines.
_____	Provide Appropriate Tools Required to Intercept and Obstruct Terrorism (PATRIOT) Act	Gives law enforcement the right to monitor people's activities, including Web and e-mail habits.
1998	_____ _____	Makes it illegal to circumvent antipiracy schemes in commercial software.
_____	National Information Infrastructure Protection Act	Penalizes theft of information across state lines, threats against networks, and computer system trespassing.
1994	Computer Abuse Amendments Act	_____ _____
1988	_____ _____	Regulates the use of government data to determine the eligibility of individuals for federal benefits.
_____	Electronic Communications Privacy Act (ECPA)	Provides the protection that covers mail and telephone communications to electronic communications.

DATE	LAW	PURPOSE
1974		Forbids federal agencies from allowing information to be used for a reason other than for which it was collected.

Things to Think About

1. Three methods of identification and authentication are user names and passwords, possessed objects, and biometric devices. What are the advantages of each method? What are the disadvantages?

2. Is it ethical to post any of the following on the Web? Why or why not?
   - material authored by someone else
   - scanned photos or pages from a book
   - song lyrics by a recording artist
   - your own or someone else's term paper

3. Should the government be allowed to access private databases or compile information from multiple departmental databases within the government? Why or why not?

4. Laws regarding information privacy, employee monitoring, and protecting children from objectionable material on the Internet remain incomplete. For which area is the need for legislation most pressing? Why?

Puzzle

All of the words described below appear in the puzzle. Words may be either forward or backward, across, up and down, or diagonal. Circle each word as you find it.

```
I  J  W  C  T  V  U  A  M  Z  Q  W  Q  Q  X  F  H  A  C  K  E  R  L  Q  Q  V  Y  P  R
G  Z  W  L  I  D  L  S  T  K  B  I  B  O  R  C  A  M  M  M  B  X  S  S  T  H  A  S  Q
Y  X  G  R  R  F  V  Y  E  Y  G  T  H  O  X  Q  Y  H  F  K  W  M  R  E  S  Y  R  C  H
W  P  U  A  B  Q  K  E  P  R  T  A  V  E  A  T  Y  J  W  T  X  P  C  H  L  N  Y  W  Q
K  S  O  T  X  T  N  M  Y  P  N  C  Y  V  P  N  P  B  T  F  P  D  A  O  O  B  C  O  L
Z  X  I  W  D  L  S  I  C  N  W  A  V  W  C  C  I  P  U  D  D  P  A  S  E  Y  C  R  K
Y  Z  M  V  S  S  I  R  K  M  H  S  M  N  N  B  C  V  E  V  D  D  T  R  S  S  D  M  B
E  D  P  D  L  C  I  C  Q  S  D  E  K  E  Q  U  I  S  Q  I  E  X  E  X  A  W  W  I  E
Y  Z  B  Z  H  F  N  R  P  M  H  O  S  Z  T  R  S  E  Z  J  K  X  I  F  P  C  O  I  R
X  A  T  Q  N  D  K  E  B  C  R  G  I  N  U  E  S  C  Y  M  T  R  E  P  E  M  D  R  B
T  R  R  V  L  D  N  B  S  T  H  U  K  S  S  I  E  G  X  O  L  G  Z  I  E  D  Y  F  D
H  H  O  G  U  U  G  Y  Q  Q  Q  K  D  S  O  N  P  D  R  O  U  E  K  T  I  J  A  S  Z
G  S  J  L  N  L  P  C  Q  W  K  E  O  N  Y  N  E  T  J  A  L  O  R  K  Y  S  V  K  Q
I  I  A  Y  T  O  O  V  P  G  F  P  Z  X  V  A  I  P  R  A  O  I  T  E  B  U  C  Q  X
R  A  N  G  M  G  I  O  L  I  Z  N  F  V  N  O  I  D  Q  C  C  P  Z  X  R  E  I  P  N
Y  U  H  O  Y  N  N  T  N  F  M  E  Z  T  N  B  H  M  S  S  I  M  E  E  O  X  P  S  O
P  D  O  Z  V  K  V  I  A  T  C  P  I  I  P  S  J  I  L  R  A  H  G  X  W  P  H  S  I
O  I  R  J  E  T  T  E  U  C  W  V  S  R  J  O  U  M  C  D  G  A  E  F  N  D  E  I  T
C  T  S  V  D  I  J  O  L  J  I  T  H  X  G  R  M  S  F  F  T  C  I  F  O  Y  R  S  A
L  T  E  G  O  T  K  U  P  R  Y  F  E  U  I  O  T  K  I  L  X  W  H  U  U  G  T  I  C
R  R  D  N  W  C  M  W  U  J  C  Y  I  C  X  N  P  R  O  K  F  I  G  Z  T  X  E  D  I
Y  A  R  A  A  S  P  S  O  H  A  N  L  T  E  C  E  V  C  E  A  V  C  Z  K  S  X  V  T
N  I  G  L  L  G  T  W  L  Z  R  J  X  D  N  W  R  T  R  Z  B  X  I  Y  W  N  T  D  N
F  L  B  R  R  W  R  S  I  G  I  B  A  B  A  E  X  S  J  E  W  K  N  F  E  M  B  T  E
W  B  J  F  A  H  O  N  E  Y  P  O  T  L  D  S  D  F  R  S  K  K  P  I  Z  N  N  F  H
A  T  T  C  F  B  M  T  N  Z  S  P  L  N  B  U  R  I  Y  S  U  C  X  V  O  Z  F  G  T
O  S  M  P  H  U  Z  X  C  N  H  A  U  U  A  R  R  K  N  E  C  V  A  R  D  A  B  R  U
L  W  D  I  Q  N  N  L  O  B  P  L  A  I  N  T  E  X  T  H  A  G  P  R  D  L  M  G  A
E  N  C  R  Y  P  T  I  O  N  K  D  X  B  R  K  N  G  K  T  H  H  O  S  C  L  B  H  P
```

Online or Internet-based illegal acts

Protective measure users take against security risks

Destructive event a virus delivers

Copies itself repeatedly, using up resources

Hides within a legitimate program

Potentially damaging program that infects a computer

Instruction saved in an application, such as a word processing program

Type of program that protects against viruses

Has the same intent as a cracker but lacks the technical skills and knowledge

Known specific pattern of virus code; sometimes called a virus signature

Someone who accesses a computer or network illegally

Someone who tries to access a computer/network illegally to perform a malicious action

Security system consisting of hardware and/or software that prevents unauthorized access to data

Outlines the computer activities for which a computer and network may and may not be used

Program designed to entice an intruder to hack into the computer

Log that records in a file all access attempts

Verifies that an individual is a valid user

Verifies that an individual is the person he or she claims to be

A private combination of characters associated with a user name that allows access to certain computer resources

A unique combination of characters that identifies a specific user

Type of device that authenticates a person's identity using physical characteristics

A numeric password

Type of object you must carry to gain access to a computer or facility

Someone who uses e-mail as a vehicle for extortion

The authorized and illegal duplication of copyrighted software

Process of converting readable data into unreadable characters to prevent unauthorized access

The unencrypted data in the encryption process

The scrambled data in the encryption process

Provides a mobile user with a secure connection to the company network server

A complete power failure

A prolonged undervoltage

Occurs when the electrical supply drops

Any unwanted signal, usually varying quickly, that is mixed with the normal voltage entering the computer

Gives authors and artists exclusive rights to duplicate, publish, and sell their materials

Small text file stored on your computer by a Web server

Self Test Answers

Matching	True/False	Multiple Choice	Fill in the Blanks
1. *e* [p. 558]	1. *F* [p. 556]	1. *d* [p. 560]	1. *cyberterrorist* [p. 557]
2. *j* [p. 558]	2. *F* [p. 561]	2. *c* [p. 561]	2. *trusted* [p. 560]
3. *g* [p. 558]	3. *T* [p. 563]	3. *c* [p. 565]	3. *inoculate* [p. 561]
4. *k* [p. 558]	4. *F* [p. 565]	4. *b* [p. 566]	4. *access* [p. 564]
5. *a* [p. 562]	5. *F* [p. 569]	5. *d* [p. 572]	5. *password* [p. 566]
6. *h* [p. 567]	6. *T* [p. 572]	6. *b* [p. 573]	6. *piracy* [p. 570]
7. *d* [p. 567]	7. *T* [p. 579]	7. *a* [p. 576]	7. *Encryption* [p. 572]
8. *i* [p. 574]	8. *T* [p. 584]	8. *a* [p. 582]	8. *backup* [p. 576]
9. *l* [p. 575]	9. *T* [p. 587]	9. *c* [p. 583]	9. *war driving* [p. 577]
10. *b* [p. 587]	10. *T* [p. 590]	10. *b* [p. 585]	10. *ethics* [p. 578]

Complete the Table

MAJOR U.S. GOVERNMENT LAWS CONCERNING PRIVACY

DATE	LAW	PURPOSE
2003	<u>*CAN-SPAM Act*</u>	Gives law enforcement the right to impose penalties on people using the Internet to distribute spam.
2002	<u>*Sarbanes-Oxley Act*</u>	Requires corporate officers, auditors, and attorneys of publicly traded companies to follow strict financial reporting guidelines.
<u>*2001*</u>	Provide Appropriate Tools Required to Intercept and Obstruct Terrorism (PATRIOT) Act	Gives law enforcement the right to monitor people's activities, including Web and e-mail habits.
1998	<u>*Digital Millennium Copyright Act (DMCA)*</u>	Makes it illegal to circumvent antipiracy schemes in commercial software.
<u>*1996*</u>	National Information Infrastructure Protection Act	Penalizes theft of information across state lines, threats against networks, and computer system trespassing.
1994	Computer Abuse Amendments Act	<u>*Amends 1984 act to outlaw transmission of harmful computer code such as viruses.*</u>

DATE	LAW	PURPOSE
1988	*Computer Matching and Privacy Protection Act*	Regulates the use of government data to determine the eligibility of individuals for federal benefits.
1986	Electronic Communications Privacy Act (ECPA)	Provides the protection that covers mail and telephone communications to electronic communications.
1974	*Privacy Act*	Forbids federal agencies from allowing information to be used for a reason other than for which it was collected.

Things to Think About

Answers will vary.

Puzzle Answer

```
I  J  W  C  T  V  U  A  M  Z  Q  W  Q  Q  X  F  H  A  C  K  E  R  L  Q  Q  V  Y  P  R
G  Z  W  L  I  D  L  S  T  K  B  I  B  O  R  C  A  M  M  M  B  X  S  S  T  H  A  S  Q
Y  X  G  R  R  F  V  Y  E  Y  G  T  H  O  X  Q  Y  H  F  K  W  M  R  E  S  Y  R  C  H
W  P  U  A  B  Q  K  E  P  R  T  A  V  E  A  T  Y  J  W  T  X  P  C  H  L  N  Y  W  Q
K  S  O  T  X  T  N  M  Y  P  N  C  Y  V  P  N  P  B  T  F  P  D  A  O  O  B  C  O  L
Z  X  I  W  D  L  S  I  C  N  W  A  W  C  C  I  P  U  D  D  P  A  S  E  Y  C  R  K
Y  Z  M  V  S  S  I  R  K  M  H  S  M  N  N  B  C  V  E  V  D  D  T  R  S  S  D  M  B
E  D  P  D  L  C  I  C  Q  S  D  E  K  E  Q  U  I  S  Q  I  E  X  E  X  A  W  I  E
Y  Z  B  Z  H  F  N  R  P  M  H  O  S  Z  T  R  S  E  Z  J  K  X  I  F  P  C  O  I  R
X  A  T  Q  N  D  K  E  B  C  R  G  I  N  U  E  S  C  Y  M  T  R  E  P  E  M  D  R  B
T  R  R  V  L  D  N  B  S  T  H  U  K  S  S  I  E  G  X  O  L  G  Z  I  E  D  Y  F  D
H  H  O  G  U  U  G  Y  Q  Q  Q  K  D  S  O  N  P  D  R  O  U  E  K  T  I  J  A  S  Z
G  S  J  L  N  L  P  C  Q  W  K  E  O  N  Y  N  E  T  J  A  L  O  R  K  Y  S  V  K  Q
I  I  A  Y  T  O  O  V  P  G  F  P  Z  X  V  A  I  P  R  A  O  I  T  E  B  U  C  Q  X
R  A  N  G  M  G  I  O  L  I  Z  N  F  V  N  O  I  D  Q  C  C  P  Z  X  R  E  I  P  N
Y  U  H  O  Y  N  N  T  N  F  M  E  Z  T  N  B  H  M  S  S  I  M  E  E  O  X  P  S  O
P  D  O  Z  V  K  V  I  A  T  C  P  I  I  P  S  J  I  L  R  A  H  G  X  W  P  H  S  I
O  I  R  J  E  T  E  U  C  W  V  S  R  J  O  U  M  C  D  G  A  E  F  N  D  E  I  T
C  T  S  V  D  I  J  O  L  J  X  T  H  X  G  R  M  S  F  F  T  C  I  F  O  Y  R  S  A
L  T  E  G  O  T  K  U  P  R  Y  F  E  U  I  O  T  K  I  L  X  W  H  U  U  G  T  I  C
R  R  D  N  W  C  M  W  U  J  C  Y  I  C  X  N  P  R  O  K  F  I  G  Z  T  X  E  D  I
Y  A  R  A  A  S  P  S  O  H  A  N  L  T  E  C  E  V  C  E  A  V  C  Z  K  S  X  V  T
N  I  G  L  L  G  T  W  L  Z  R  J  X  D  N  W  R  T  R  Z  B  X  I  Y  W  N  T  D  N
F  L  B  R  R  W  R  S  I  G  I  B  A  B  A  E  X  S  J  E  W  K  N  F  E  M  B  T  E
W  B  J  F  A  H  O  N  E  Y  P  O  T  L  D  S  D  F  R  S  K  K  P  I  Z  N  N  F  H
A  T  T  C  F  B  M  T  N  Z  S  P  L  N  B  U  R  I  Y  S  U  C  X  V  O  Z  F  G  T
O  S  M  P  H  U  Z  X  C  N  H  A  U  U  A  R  R  K  N  E  C  V  A  R  D  A  B  R  U
L  W  D  I  Q  N  N  L  O  B  P  L  A  I  N  T  E  X  T  H  A  G  P  R  D  L  M  G  A
E  N  C  R  Y  P  T  I  O  N  K  D  X  B  R  K  N  G  K  T  H  H  O  S  C  L  B  H  P
```

DISCOVERING COMPUTERS 2007
STUDY GUIDE

CHAPTER 12
Information System Development

Chapter Overview

This chapter discusses the phases in the system development cycle. The guidelines for system development also are presented. The chapter also addresses activities that occur during the entire system development cycle including project management, feasibility assessment, data and information gathering, and documentation. Throughout the chapter, a case study about Web Stop Café illustrates and reinforces activities performed during each phase of the system development cycle.

Chapter Objectives

After completing this chapter, you should be able to:

- List the phases in the system development cycle
- Identify the guidelines for system development
- Discuss the importance of project management, feasibility assessment, documentation, and data and information gathering techniques
- Explain the activities performed in the planning phase
- Discuss the purpose of the activities performed in the analysis phase
- Describe the various tools used in process modeling
- Describe the various tools used in object modeling
- Explain the activities performed in the design phase
- Recognize that the develop programs activity is part of the system development cycle
- Discuss the activities performed in the implementation phase
- Discuss the purpose of the activities performed in the operation, support, and security phase

Chapter Outline

I. What is the system development cycle? [p. 620]

A system is _____

_____

An information system (IS) is _____

_____

The system development cycle is _____

_____

A. Phases in the system development cycle [p. 620]

A phase is _____

Most system development cycles contain five phases:

1. _____   3. _____   5. _____

2. _____   4. _____

The phases form a loop; that is, information system development is an
ongoing process.

B. Guidelines for system development [p. 621]

System development should follow three general guidelines:

(1) _____

(2) _____

Users include _____

_____

(3) _____

Standards are _____

_____

C. Who participates in the system development cycle? [p. 622]

A systems analyst is _____

_____

A system developer is _____

_____

The steering committee is_____

_____

A project team is_____

_____

The project leader manages _____

_____

D. Project management [p. 623]

Project management is _____

_____

To plan and schedule a project effectively, the project leader identifies:

•   _____

The scope of a project is _____

_____

- _____
- _____
- _____
- _____
- _____

The project leader usually records these items in a project plan.

A Gantt chart is _____

_____

Scope creep is _____

_____

Change management skills allow _____

_____

A deliverable is _____

_____

Project leaders can use project management software to _____

_____

E. Feasibility assessment [p. 625]
    Feasibility is _____

_____

Criteria used to test project feasibility:

- Operational feasibility measures _____

_____

- Schedule feasibility measures_____

_____

- Technical feasibility measures _____

_____

- Economic feasibility, or cost/benefit feasibility, measures _____

_____

F. Documentation [p. 625]
    Documentation is _____

_____

A project notebook contains _____

_____

Well-written, thorough, and understandable documentation makes it easier to work with and modify existing systems.

G. Data and information gathering techniques [p. 625]

Techniques used during the system development cycle to gather data and information:

- _____
- _____
- _____
- _____
- _____

A joint-application design (JAD) session is _____

_____

- _____

II. What initiates the system development cycle? [p. 626]

A user may request a new or modified information system for a variety of reasons, such as to correct a problem, to comply with a mandated change, or to respond to competitors.

A request for system services, or project request, is a formal request for a new or modified information system and becomes _____

_____

III. Planning phase [p. 629]

The planning phase begins _____

_____

Major activities during the planning phase:

(1) _____
(2) _____
(3) _____
(4) _____

IV. Analysis phase [p. 630]

The analysis phase consists of two major activities:

(1) _____
(2) _____

A. The preliminary investigation [p. 630]

The preliminary investigation (or feasibility study) is _____

_____

In this phase, the systems analyst defines _____

A feasibility study presents the results of the preliminary investigation.

B. Detailed analysis [p. 631]

Detailed analysis involves three major activities:

(1) _____

(2) _____

(3) _____

Detailed analysis sometimes is called logical design because _____

_____

C. Process modeling [p. 632]

Process modeling (or structured analysis and design) is _____

_____

1. Entity-relationship diagrams [p. 632]

An entity-relationship diagram (ERD) is _____

_____

An entity is _____

_____

2. Data flow diagrams [p. 632]

A data flow diagram (DFD) is _____

_____

Components of a DFD:

• A data flow shows _____

• A process transforms _____

• A data store is _____

• A source identifies _____

A context diagram (the top level DFD) identifies _____

_____

3. Project dictionary [p. 633]

The project dictionary (or repository) contains _____

_____

In the project dictionary, entries from DFDs and ERDs are described using
several techniques, including structured English, decision tables and
decision trees, and the data dictionary.

Structured English is _____

_____

A decision table is _____

A decision tree shows _____

The data dictionary section of the project dictionary stores _____

D. Object modeling [p. 635]

Object modeling, sometimes called object-oriented (OO) analysis and design, combines _____

An object is _____

An attribute (or property) is _____

An operation (or method) is _____

UML (Unified Modeling Language) is _____

The Rational Unified Process (RUP) is _____

1. Use case diagram [p. 636]
   A use case diagram shows _____

   An actor is _____

   The use case is _____

2. Class diagram [p. 636]
   A class diagram shows _____

   Subclasses are _____

   Inheritance is _____

E. The system proposal [p. 636]
   The system proposal assesses _____

When discussing the system proposal, the steering committee often must decide whether to buy packaged software, build custom software, or hire an outside firm to handle some or all of its IT needs.

1. Packaged software [p. 637]

   Packaged software is _____

   _____

   • Horizontal market software is _____

   _____

   • Vertical market software is _____

   _____

   Sources of packaged software can be found on the Web or in trade publications. A trade publication is _____

   _____

2. Custom software [p. 637]

   Custom software is _____

   _____

   The advantage of custom software is _____

   _____

   The disadvantages of custom software are _____

   _____

3. Outsourcing [p. 637]

   To outsource means _____

   _____

   An Internet solutions provider is _____

   _____

V. Design phase [p. 639]

   The design phase consists of two major activities:

   (1) _____

   (2) _____

   A. Acquiring necessary hardware and software [p. 639]

      Acquiring the necessary hardware and software consists of four tasks:

      (1) _____

      (2) _____

      (3) _____

      (4) _____

B. Identifying technical specifications [p. 639]

A systems analyst uses a variety of techniques to identify the hardware and software requirements for a system, such as researching on the Internet.

An e-zine (or electronic magazine) is _____

_____

Technical requirements are summarized using three basic techniques:

- A request for quotation (RFQ) identifies _____

_____

- A request for proposal (RFP) selects _____

_____

- A request for information (RFI) is _____

_____

The RFQ, RFP, and RFI are sent to potential hardware and software vendors.

C. Soliciting vendor proposals [p. 639]

Proposals can be solicited from vendors on the Internet, local computer stores, computer manufacturers, or value-added resellers.

A value-added reseller (VAR) is _____

_____

A VAR may offer user support, equipment maintenance, training, installation, warranties, and turnkey solutions.

A turnkey solution is _____

_____

An IT consultant is _____

_____

D. Testing and evaluating vendor proposals [p. 640]

A benchmark test measures _____

_____

E. Making a decision [p. 640]

After rating proposals, the systems analyst makes a recommendation to the steering committee. A contract then can be awarded to a vendor.

F. Detailed design [p. 641]

A detailed design sometimes is called a physical design because _____

_____

Designs are developed for databases, inputs, outputs, and programs.

1. Database design [p. 641]

During database design, the systems analyst builds _____

2. Input and output design [p. 641]

    During input and output design, the systems analyst designs _____

    _____

    •   A mockup is _____

        _____

    •   A layout chart is _____

        _____

3. Program design [p. 642]

    During program design, the systems analyst prepares _____

    _____

    The program specification package identifies _____

    _____

G. Prototyping [p. 642]

    A prototype is _____

    _____

H. CASE tools [p. 642]

    Computer-aided software engineering (CASE) products are _____

    _____

    Capabilities of integrated CASE (sometimes called I-CASE or a CASE
    workbench) products:

    •   _____   •   _____

    •   _____   •   _____

    •   _____   •   _____

I. Quality review techniques [p. 643]

    An inspection is _____

    _____

VI. Implementation phase [p. 643]

    The purpose of the implementation phase is _____

    _____

    Four major activities are performed in the implementation phase:

    (1) _____

    (2) _____

    (3) _____

(4) _____

A. Develop programs [p. 643]

Custom software can be developed from the specifications created during analysis using a set of activities known as the program development cycle. The program development cycle is_____

_____

The program development cycle follows six steps:

(1) _____   (4) _____

(2) _____   (5) _____

(3) _____   (6) _____

B. Install and test the new system [p. 644]

Types of tests performed to test the new system:

- A unit test verifies _____

_____

- A systems test verifies _____

_____

- An integration test verifies _____

_____

- An acceptance test checks _____

_____

C. Train users [p. 644]

Training involves _____

_____

D. Convert to the new system [p. 644]

Conversion can take place using the following strategies:

- With direct conversion (or abrupt cutover), the user stops _____

_____

- With parallel conversion, the old system runs _____

_____

- With a phased conversion, each site converts _____

_____

- With a pilot conversion, only one location uses _____

_____

Data conversion is _____

_____

VII. Operation, support, and security phase [p. 646]

The purpose of the operation, support, and security phase is _____

_____

The support phase consists of four major activities:

(1) _____

(2) _____

(3) _____

The post-implementation system review is _____

_____

Corrective maintenance is _____

_____

Adaptive maintenance is _____

_____

Performance monitoring is _____

_____

Perfective maintenance is _____

_____

A chief security officer (CSO) is responsible for _____

_____

A. Developing a computer security plan [p. 646]

A computer security plan summarizes _____

_____

A computer security plan should do the following:

(1) _____

(2) _____

(3) _____

Companies and individuals that need help with computer security plans
can contact the International Computer Security Association (ICSA) Labs
for assistance.

Self Test

Matching

1. ____	IS	a. a meeting in which users and IT professionals work to design and develop an application
2. ____	JAD	
3. ____	ERD	b. standard form sent to vendors to request information about a product or service
4. ____	DFD	
5. ____	UML	c. company that purchases products and resells them along with additional services
6. ____	RFQ	d. a graphical tool that enables analysts to document a system
7. ____	RFP	
8. ____	RFI	e. hardware, software, data, people, and procedures that work together to produce quality information
9. ____	VAR	
10. ____	CASE	f. license agreement granting the right to use software under certain terms and conditions

g. tool that graphically shows the flow of data in a system

h. sent to vendors to identify the products you want and request prices

i. tabular representation of actions to be taken given various conditions

j. software tools designed to support activities of the system development cycle

k. tool that graphically shows the connections between entities in a system

l. asks vendors to select products that meet your requirements and then quote prices

True/False

____ 1. The goal of project management is to deliver an acceptable system to the user in an agreed-upon time frame, while maintaining costs.

____ 2. Documentation should be an ongoing part of the system development cycle.

____ 3. The interview is the least important data and information gathering technique.

____ 4. The problem suggested in the project request always is the actual problem.

____ 5. An important benefit from using all of the data and information gathering techniques is that these activities build valuable relationships among the systems analyst and users.

_____ 6. Lower-level data flow diagrams (DFDs) identify only the major process; that is, the system being studied.

_____ 7. Vertical market software packages tend to be widely available as many companies use them, so they usually are cheaper than horizontal market software packages.

_____ 8. To be an authorized VAR, most manufacturers have requirements the VAR must meet.

_____ 9. The main advantage of a prototype is that users can work with the system before it is completed — to make sure it meets their needs.

_____ 10. Errors in a system in which the program does not produce correct results are usually the result of problems with design (logic).

Multiple Choice

_____ 1. Which of the following is *not* a general guideline for system development?
   a. set constraints
   b. use phases
   c. involve users
   d. develop standards

_____ 2. What criterion that tests the feasibility of a project addresses the question of whether users will like the new system?
   a. cost/benefit feasibility
   b. technical feasibility
   c. schedule feasibility
   d. operational feasibility

_____ 3. What is a reason for requesting a new or modified information system?
   a. comply with a mandated change
   b. respond to competitors
   c. correct a problem
   d. all of the above

_____ 4. The preliminary investigation is a major task in what phase?
   a. analysis
   b. planning
   c. design
   d. implementation

_____ 5. In a data flow diagram, what is drawn as a circle?
   a. data flow
   b. process
   c. data store
   d. source

_____ 6. What technique graphically represents a variety of conditions and the actions that correspond to each?
   a. project dictionary
   b. decision tree
   c. data dictionary
   d. decision table

_____ 7. What is the main advantage of custom software?
   a. it matches an organization's requirements exactly
   b. it is less expensive than packaged software
   c. it takes less time to design than packaged software
   d. it takes less time to implement than packaged software

_____ 8. Which of the following identify the required programs for the programmer?
   a. prototype
   b. layout chart
   c. mockup
   d. program specification package

_____ 9. What capability is *not* included in I-CASE products?
   a. graphics that enable the drawing of diagrams
   b. quality assurance that analyzes deliverables
   c. generators that produce design specifications from actual programs
   d. prototypes that create models of a proposed system

_____ 10. An accounting system, with its constituent sites all being converted in separate stages, would be an example of what kind of conversion?
   a. direct conversion
   b. parallel conversion
   c. phased conversion
   d. pilot conversion

Fill in the Blanks

1. To help organize the process, system development cycles often group many activities into larger categories called _____.

2. To plan and schedule a project effectively, the project leader must identify the goal, objectives, and expectations of the project, called the _____.

3. A document called a(n) _____ becomes the first item in the project notebook and triggers the first phase in the system development cycle.

4. A report called a(n) _____ compiles the findings of a very general preliminary investigation.

5. In a data flow diagram, a(n) _____ identifies an entity outside the scope of the system that sends data into or receives information from the system.

6. The goal of the _____ is to assess the feasibility of each alternative solution and recommend the most feasible solution for the development project.

7. _____ is application software developed by the user or at the user's request.

8. Companies can develop software in-house using their own IT personnel or _____ it, which means having an outside source develop it for them.

9. _____ users to use the new hardware and software in a system could be one-on-one sessions or classroom-style lectures.

10. Converting existing manual and computer files so they can be used by a new system is known as _____.

Complete the Table

CONVERTING TO A NEW SYSTEM

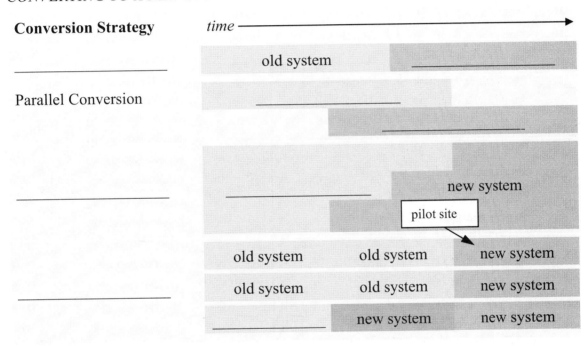

Conversion Strategy	time ⟶
_____	old system ⟶ _____
Parallel Conversion	_____ ⟶ _____
_____	_____ ⟶ new system (pilot site ⟶ new system)
_____	old system / old system / new system; old system / old system / new system; _____ / new system / new system

Things to Think About

1. Why does the start of many activities in the system development cycle depend on the successful completion of other activities?

2. Although they are created in the analysis phase, how might the project dictionary and data dictionary be used in subsequent phases of the system development cycle?

3. If an organization chooses to buy packaged software, why might it have to change some of its methods and procedures? When might custom software be worth the additional cost and development time?

4. How can untrained users prevent the estimated benefits of a new system from ever being obtained or, worse, contribute to less efficiency and more costs than when the old system was operational?

Puzzle

Write the word described by each clue in the puzzle below. Words can be written forward or backward, across, up and down, or diagonally. The initial letter of each word already appears in the puzzle.

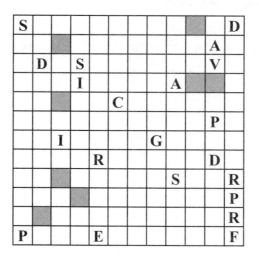

Sets of rules and procedures a company expects employees to follow

Formed to work on a development project from beginning to end

Type of horizontal bar chart that shows time relationship of project activities

Tangible item such as a chart, diagram, report, or program file

Measure of how suitable development of a system will be to a company

Phase in which the project request is reviewed and approved

Phase in which detailed analysis is performed

Tool that graphically shows connections between entities in a project

Tool that graphically shows the flow of data in a system

In a data flow diagram, it is represented by a line with an arrow

In a data flow diagram, it is represented by a rectangle with no sides

In a data flow diagram, it is represented by a square

Contains all the documentation and deliverables of a project

Type of software developed by the user or at the user's request

Identifies the products you want from a vendor

Vendor selection of products that meet requirements

Less formal method that uses a standard form to request product information

Company that purchases products and resells them with additional services

Working model of a proposed system used during detailed design

Type of conversion in which only one location uses the new system

Phase in which a post-implementation system review is conducted

Hardware, software, data, people, and procedures that work together to produce quality information

Where a project leader records a project's goals and required activities, for example

Type of professionals that work with users during a JAD session

A user or other entity in a use case diagram

Self Test Answers

Matching	True/False	Multiple Choice	Fill in the Blanks
1. *e* [p. 620]	1. *T* [p. 623]	1. *a* [p. 621]	1. *phases* [p. 620]
2. *a* [p. 626]	2. *T* [p. 625]	2. *d* [p. 625]	2. *scope* [p. 623]
3. *k* [p. 632]	3. *F* [p. 626]	3. *d* [p. 626]	3. *request for system services* or *project request* [p. 627]
4. *g* [p. 632]	4. *F* [p. 630]	4. *a* [p. 630]	4. *feasibility study* [p. 630]
5. *d* [p. 635]	5. *T* [p. 631]	5. *b* [p. 632]	5. *source* [p. 632]
6. *h* [p. 639]	6. *F* [p. 633]	6. *b* [p. 634]	6. *system proposal* [p. 636]
7. *l* [p. 639]	7. *F* [p. 637]	7. *a* [p. 637]	7. *Custom software* [p. 637]
8. *b* [p. 639]	8. *T* [p. 639]	8. *d* [p. 642]	8. *outsource* [p. 637]
9. *c* [p. 639]	9. *T* [p. 642]	9. *c* [p. 643]	9. *Training* [p. 644]
10. *j* [p. 642]	10. *T* [p. 646]	10. *c* [p. 645]	10. *data conversion* [p. 645]

Complete the Table

CONVERTING TO A NEW SYSTEM

Conversion Strategy	time ⟶		
Direct Conversion	old system	*new system*	
Parallel Conversion	*old system*		
		new system	
Phased Conversion	*old system*	new system	
	pilot site		
	old system	old system	new system
Pilot Conversion	old system	old system	new system
	new system	new system	new system

Things to Think About

Answers will vary.

Puzzle Answer

S	T	A	N	D	A	R	D	S		R	D
N	Y		S	I	S	Y	L	A	N	A	E
A	D	T	S	U	P	P	O	R	T	V	P
L	A	F	I	R	O	T	C	A			Y
P	T		D	L	C	U	S	T	O	M	T
T	A	I	T	Q	I	T	O	L	I	P	O
C	F	I	F	F	O	B	G	A	N	T	T
E	L	B	A	R	E	V	I	L	E	D	O
J	O		E	C	R	U	O	S	P	F	R
O	W	D		G	N	I	N	N	A	L	P
R		Y	R	O	T	I	S	O	P	E	R
P	R	O	J	E	C	T	T	E	A	M	F

Notes

DISCOVERING COMPUTERS 2007

STUDY GUIDE

CHAPTER 13

Programming Languages and Program Development

Chapter Overview

This chapter explains various programming languages used to write and develop computer programs. It also presents a variety of Web development and multimedia development tools. Finally, the chapter describes each step in the program development cycle and presents the tools used to make this process efficient.

Chapter Objectives

After completing this chapter, you should be able to:

- Differentiate between machine and assembly languages
- Identify and discuss the purpose of procedural programming languages
- Identify and discuss the characteristics of object-oriented programming languages and program development tools
- Identify the uses of other programming languages and other program development tools
- Describe various ways to develop Web pages, including HTML,

scripting languages, DHTML, XML, WML, and Web page authoring software
- Identify the uses of popular multimedia authoring programs
- List the six steps in the program development cycle
- Differentiate between structured design and object-oriented design
- Explain the basic control structures and design tools used in designing solutions to programming problems

Chapter Outline

I. Computer programs and programming languages [p. 664]

A computer program is _____

_____

A computer programmer (or developer) is _____

_____

A programming language is _____

To code means _____

A low-level language is _____

A machine-dependent language runs _____

A high-level language is _____

A machine-independent language can _____

II. Low-level languages [p. 665]
Machine language is _____

An assembly language is _____

Symbolic instruction codes are _____

A symbolic address is _____

To execute a program means _____

A source program is _____

An assembler is _____

A macro generates _____

III. Procedural languages [p. 666]
A procedural language is _____

A third-generation language (3GL) is _____

A compiler is _____

The object code (or object program) is _____

_____

An interpreter is _____

_____

An algorithm is _____

_____

   A. COBOL [p. 668]

      COBOL (COmmon Business-Oriented Language) is _____

      _____

      Grace Hopper was_____

      _____

      Micro Focus is _____

      _____

   B. C [p. 668]

      C is _____

      _____

IV. Object-oriented programming languages and program development tools [p. 669]

    An object-oriented programming (OOP) language is used _____

    _____

    A program development tool is _____

    _____

    An object is _____

    _____

    An event is _____

    _____

    An event-driven program checks _____

    _____

    RAD (rapid application development) is _____

    _____

   A. Java [p. 669]

      Java is _____

      _____

      Bytecode is _____

      _____

      A just-in-time (JIT) compiler is _____

J2EE (Java 2 Platform Enterprise Edition) is _____

_____

B. C++ [p. 670]

C++ is _____

_____

C. C# [p. 670]

C# is _____

_____

Microsoft Intermediate Language (MSIL) is _____

_____

D. Visual Studio 2005 [p. 670]

Visual Studio 2005 is _____

_____

.NET is _____

Code snippets are_____

Visual Basic 2005 is _____

_____

Visual C++ 2005 is _____

_____

Visual C# 2005 is _____

_____

Visual J# 2005 is_____

_____

E. Delphi [p. 672]

Delphi is _____

_____

F. PowerBuilder [p. 673]

PowerBuilder is _____

_____

G. Visual programming languages [p. 673]

A visual programming language is _____

_____

A visual programming environment (VPE) allows _____

_____

V. Other programming languages [p. 674]

A. RPG [p. 674]

RPG (Report Program Generator) is _____

_____

B. 4GLs [p. 674]

A 4GL (fourth-generation language) is _____

_____

A nonprocedural language is _____

_____

SQL is _____

_____

C. Classic programming languages [p. 675]

Some of the languages listed in Figure 13-15 on page 675, although once popular, find little use today.

VI. Other program development tools [p. 676]

A. Application generators [p. 676]

An application generator is _____

_____

A report writer is _____

_____

A form is _____

_____

A menu generator is _____

_____

B. Macros [p. 676]

A macro is _____

A macro recorder is _____

_____

Many programs use Visual Basic for Applications (VBA) or a similar language as their macro programming language.

VII. Web page development [p. 678]

Web page authors use _____

A. HTML [p. 678]

HTML (Hypertext Markup Language) is _____

_____

HTML uses tags, which are _____

_____

B. Scripts, applets, servlets, and ActiveX controls [p. 679]

To add dynamic content and interactive elements to Web pages, you write small programs called scripts, applets, servlets, and ActiveX controls.

- A script is _____
- An applet usually runs _____
- A servlet is _____
- An ActiveX control is _____
  ActiveX is _____

Interactive capabilities on a Web page:

- A counter tracks _____
- An image map is _____
- A processing form collects _____

The CGI (common gateway interface) is _____

_____

A CGI script is _____

C. Scripting languages [p. 680]

A scripting language is _____

_____

Popular scripting languages:

JavaScript is _____

_____

A mouse rollover or mouseover occurs when _____

_____

An open language means _____

_____

Perl (Practical Extraction and Report Language) is _____

_____

Rexx (REstructured eXtended eXecutor) _____

_____

Tcl (Tool Command Language) _____

_____

VBScript (Visual Basic, Scripting Edition) is _____

_____

D. Dynamic HTML [p. 682]

Dynamic HTML (DHTML) is _____

_____

Dynamic HTML works by using the document object model, style sheets, and scripting languages.

- The document object model (DOM) defines _____

_____

- A style sheet contains _____

- Cascading style sheets (CSS) contain _____

_____

E. XHTML, XML, and WML [p. 682]

XHTML (eXtensible HTML) includes features of HTML and XML.

XML (eXtensible Markup Language) is_____

_____

RSS 2.0 (Really Simple Syndication)_____

_____

WML (wireless markup language) allows _____

_____

F. Ajax [p. 683]

Ajax is _____

_____

G. Web page authoring software [p. 683]

Web page authoring software allows _____

_____

Three popular Web page authoring programs are:

- Dreamweaver MX is_____

_____

- Flash MX is _____

_____

- FrontPage is _____

_____

VIII. Multimedia program development [p. 684]

Multimedia authoring software allows _____

_____

Many developers use multimedia authoring software for computer-based training

(CBT) and Web-based training (WBT).

ToolBook has _____

_____

Authorware is _____

_____

Director MX is _____

_____

IX. The program development cycle [p. 685]

The program development cycle is _____

_____

The program development cycle consists of six steps:

1. _____ 3. _____ 5. _____

2. _____ 4. _____ 6. _____

The phases form a loop; that is, program development is an ongoing process within system development.

To maintain a program means _____

_____

   A. What initiates the program development cycle? [p. 686]

     A company may opt for in-house development of custom software, purchasing package software, or outsourcing some or all of the IT operation.

     The program development cycle begins at the start of the implementation phase of the system development cycle.

     A programming team consists of _____

     _____

X. Step 1 – Analyze requirements [p. 686]

The analysis step consists of three major tasks:

(1) _____

(2) _____

(3) _____

An IPO chart identifies _____

_____

XI. Step 2 – Design solution [p. 687]

A solution algorithm, also called program logic, is _____

_____

A. Structured design [p. 687]

   Structured (or top-down) design begins _____

   _____

   • The main routine or main module is _____

   _____

   • Subroutines or modules are _____

   _____

   A hierarchy chart, also called a structure chart, shows _____

   _____

B. Object-oriented design [p. 688]

   Object-oriented (OO) design is _____

   _____

   Encapsulation is _____

   _____

C. Control structures [p. 688]

   A control structure (or construct) is _____

   _____

   Structured design and object-oriented design use three basic control structures
   — sequence, selection, and repetition.

   1. Sequence control structure [p. 688]

      A sequence control structure shows _____

      _____

   2. Selection control structure [p. 689]

      A selection control structure tells _____

      _____

      Common types of selection control structures:

      • An if-then-else control structure yields _____

      _____

      • The case control structure can yield _____

      _____

   3. Repetition control structure [p. 689]

      The repetition control structure enables _____

      _____

      A loop is _____

      Forms of the repetition control structure:

- The do-while control structure repeats _____

  _____

- The do-until control structure is _____

  _____

D. Design tools [p. 690]

Design tools help to document a solution algorithm. Two design tools are program flowcharts and pseudocode.

A program flowchart, or simply flowchart, graphically shows _____

_____

A comment symbol, or an annotation symbol, explains _____

_____

Programmers use flowcharting software to develop flowcharts.

Pseudocode uses _____

_____

XII. Step 3 – Validate design [p. 693]

To validate program design means _____

_____

A logic error is _____

_____

A desk check is _____

_____

Test data is _____

_____

XIII. Step 4 – Implement design [p. 693]

Implementation includes _____

_____

Coding involves _____

_____

Syntax is _____

Comments are _____

_____

- Global comments explain _____

- Internal comments explain _____

A. Extreme programming [p. 695]

Extreme programming (XP) is _____

_____

XIV.   Step 5 – Test solution [p. 695]

The goal of program testing is _____

_____

Errors usually are one of two types:

(1) _____   (2) _____

A syntax error occurs _____

A run-time error is _____

If an expected result and actual result do not match, the program has a logic error.

Debugging is _____

Bugs are _____

A debug utility, or debugger, allows _____

_____

A beta is _____

_____

XV.   Step 6 – Document solution [p. 696]

In documenting the solution, the programmer performs two activities:

(1) _____

(2) _____

Dead code is _____

_____

Self Test

Matching

1. _____ COBOL
2. _____ C
3. _____ Java
4. _____ C++
5. _____ Delphi
6. _____ RPG
7. _____ HTML
8. _____ VBScript
9. _____ Perl
10. _____ XML

a. an extension of C

b. introduced by IBM to assist businesses in generating reports

c. scientific language designed to manipulate tables of numbers

d. object-oriented language developed by Apple to manipulate multimedia cards

e. powerful visual programming tool ideal for large-scale enterprise application development

f. interpreted scripting language with powerful text processing capabilities

g. scripting language used to add intelligence and interactivity to Web pages

h. widely used procedural language for business applications

i. originally designed as a language for writing systems software, most often used with UNIX

j. object-oriented programming language developed by Sun Microsystems

k. special formatting language that programmers use to create Web pages

l. markup language that allows developers to create customized tags or use predefined tags

True/False

_____ 1. A high-level language is a programming language that is machine dependent.

_____ 2. With a machine language, the second generation of programming languages, a programmer writes instructions using symbolic instruction codes.

_____ 3. A major benefit of OOP is the ability to reuse and modify existing objects.

_____ 4. RAD is a method of developing software, in which the programmer writes and implements a program in segments instead of waiting until the entire program is completed.

_____ 5. A compiler creates source code from a required functionality's specification.

_____ 6. JavaScript is a closed language; no one can use it without a license.

_____   7. In structured design, a programmer begins with a general design and moves toward a more detailed design.

_____   8. A do-while control structure tests the condition at the end of the loop.

_____   9. Extreme programming has programmers beginning to code and test solutions as soon as requirements are defined.

_____ 10. Widow code is any program instructions that a program never executes.

Multiple Choice

_____   1. Which of the following types of languages is the only language the computer directly recognizes?
  a. procedural
  b. assembly
  c. machine
  d. object-oriented

_____   2. Which of the following converts the entire source program into machine language before executing it?
  a. compiler
  b. translator
  c. interpreter
  d. executor

_____   3. Which of the following is an action to which a program responds?
  a. procedure
  b. function
  c. method
  d. event

_____   4. What is the name of Microsoft's latest suite of visual programming languages and RAD tools?
  a. Delphi 2005
  b. PowerBuilder 2005
  c. Visual Basic 2005
  d. Visual Studio 2005

_____   5. What are statements instructing an application how to complete a task called?
  a. macros
  b. applets
  c. tags
  d. scripts

_____   6. Which of the following runs on the client, but is compiled?
  a. ActiveX control
  b. macro
  c. script
  d. applet

_____ 7. Which of these multimedia authoring applications includes Lingo?
   a. ToolBook
   b. Director
   c. Authorware
   d. all of the above

_____ 8. Which step in the program development cycle includes the identification of input, output, processing, and data components?
   a. implementation
   b. analysis
   c. support
   d. design

_____ 9. In which structure can a condition yield one of three or more possibilities?
   a. do-while control structure
   b. sequence control structure
   c. case control structure
   d. do-until control structure

_____ 10. Which of these is designed to identify errors in the program logic?
   a. audit trail
   b. desk check
   c. pseudocode
   d. syntax validation

Fill in the Blanks

1. A programming _____ is a set of words, symbols, and codes that enables a programmer to communicate instructions to a computer.

2. In a(n) _____ language, the programmer assigns a name to a program-instruction sequence that tells the computer what to do and how to do it.

3. With a(n) _____ language, the programmer writes English-like instructions that retrieve data from files or a database.

4. HTML _____ are codes that indicate how a Web page displays.

5. A(n) _____ contains descriptions of a document's characteristics.

6. A(n) _____ algorithm is a graphical or written description of the step-by-step procedures to solve a problem.

7. The concept of packaging data and procedures into a single object is called

   _____.

8. A(n) _____ graphically shows the logic in a solution algorithm.

9. A(n) _____ error occurs when the code violates the syntax, or grammar, of the programming language.

10. A(n) _____ is a program that has most or all of its features and functionality implemented.

Complete the Table

ANSI FLOWCHART SYMBOLS

Symbol	Operation/Purpose
☐	_____ program instruction(s) that transforms input(s) into output(s) INPUT/OUTPUT: _____
- - - ⌐	_____ additional descriptive information about the program
◇	_____ condition that determines a specified path to follow TERMINAL: _____
○	_____ entry from or exit to another part of the flowchart on the same page CONNECTOR: _____
▯	_____ named process containing a series of program steps specified elsewhere

Things to Think About

1. Why should a programmer not change design specifications without the agreement of the systems analyst and the user?

2. Prior to the introduction of structured program design, programmers focused on the detailed steps required for a program and logical solutions for each new combination of conditions as it was encountered. Why would developing programs in this manner lead to these poorly designed programs?

3. Why is it better to find errors and make needed changes to a program during the design step than to make them later in the development process?

4. Would it be more difficult to uncover syntax errors or logic errors in a program? Why?

Puzzle

The terms described by the phrases below are written below each line in code. Break the code by writing the correct term above the coded word. Then, use your broken code to translate the final sentence.

1. Series of instructions that directs the computer to perform tasks

   _____
   EJGCWMZD CDJUDHG

2. Includes writing the code that translates the design into a program and creating the user interface

   _____
   SGCVZGZBMHMSJB

3. Type of language in which each instruction equates to multiple machine instructions

   _____
   YSUY-VZKZV

4. Technique in which the programmer builds from a general design toward a more detailed one

   _____
   QMDWEMWDZI IZQSUB

5. Design that determines the logical order of program instructions

   _____
   EJBQMDWEM

6. Type of control structure that shows one or more actions following each other in order

   _____
   QZXWZBEZ

7. Type of control structure used when a program performs one or more actions repeatedly

   _____
   DZCZMSMSJB

8. A language's set of grammar and rules specifying how to write instructions for an algorithm

   _____
   QPBMHL

9. Design tool that uses a condensed form of English to convey program logic

   _____
   CQZWIJEJIZ

10. Utility that identifies syntax errors and finds logic errors in a program

    _____
    IZAWUUZD

11. The use of test data to step through the logic of a solution algorithm

    _____
    IZQF EYZEF

12. Another name for a comment symbol

    _____
    HBBJMHMSJB QPGAJV

13. Control structure that repeats one or more times as long as a condition is true

    _____
    IJ-RYSVZ

14. Series of steps programmers use to build computer programs

    _____
    CDJUDHG IZKZVJCGZBM EPEVZ

15. Borland's powerful visual programming tool that is ideal for large-scale development

IZVCYS _____

16. HTML codes that specify links to other documents and how a Web page displays

MHUQ _____

17. Collects data from visitors to a Web site, who fill in blank fields

CDJEZQQSBU OJDG _____

18. Simple, open scripting language that anyone can use without purchasing a license

THKHQEDSCM _____

19. Web page development language that can be used to define a link to multiple Web sites

ZLMZBQSAVZ GHDFWC _____

MJ VWDZ ZLCZDM CDJUDHGGZDQ, SB HIISMSJB MJ YSUY QHVHDSZQ HBI

QSUBSBU AJBWQZQ QJGZ EJGCHBSZQ JOOZD QWEY CZDFQ HQ

OVZLSAVZ YJWDQ, IHP EHDZ, OHGSVP VZHKZ, QMJEF JCMSJBQ, RJDFCVHEZ

OSMBZQQ EZBMZDQ, HBI ZKZB VHWBIDP QZDKSEZ.

Self Test Answers

Matching	True/False	Multiple Choice	Fill in the Blanks
1. *h* [p. 668]	1. *F* [p. 665]	1. *c* [p. 665]	1. *language* [p. 664]
2. *i* [p. 668]	2. *F* [p. 666]	2. *a* [p. 666]	2. *procedural* [p. 666]
3. *j* [p. 669]	3. *T* [p. 669]	3. *d* [p. 669]	3. *nonprocedural* [p. 674]
4. *a* [p. 670]	4. *T* [p. 670]	4. *d* [p. 670]	4. *tags* [p. 678]
5. *e* [p. 672]	5. *F* [p. 676]	5. *a* [p. 676]	5. *style sheet* [p. 682]
6. *b* [p. 674]	6. *F* [p. 681]	6. *d* [p. 679]	6. *solution* [p. 687]
7. *k* [p. 678]	7. *T* [p. 687]	7. *b* [p. 684]	7. *encapsulation* [p. 688]
8. *g* [p. 681]	8. *F* [p. 689]	8. *b* [p. 686]	8. *program flowchart* or *flowchart* [p. 690]
9. *f* [p. 681]	9. *T* [p. 695]	9. *c* [p. 689]	9. *syntax* [p. 695]
10. *l* [p. 682]	10. *F* [p. 696]	10. *b* [p. 693]	10. *beta* [p. 696]

Complete the Table

ANSI FLOWCHART SYMBOLS

Symbol	Operation/Purpose
▭	*PROCESS:* program instruction(s) that transforms input(s) into output(s)
▱	INPUT/OUTPUT: *enter data or display information*
⊏ (dashed)	*ANNOTATION:* additional descriptive information about the program
◇	*DECISION:* condition that determines a specified path to follow
⬭	TERMINAL: *beginning or ending of program*
◯	*CONNECTOR:* entry from or exit to another part of the flowchart on the same page

Symbol	Operation/Purpose
	CONNECTOR: *entry from or exit to another part of the flowchart on a different page*
	PREDEFINED PROCESS: named process containing a series of program steps specified elsewhere

Things to Think About

Answers will vary.

Puzzle Answer

1. Set of instructions that directs the computer to perform tasks

    computer program
    EJGCWMZD CDJUDHG

2. Includes writing the code that translates the design into a program and creating the user interface

    implementation
    SGCVZGZBMHMSJB

3. Type of language in which each instruction equates to multiple machine instructions

    high-level
    YSUY-VZKZV

4. Technique in which the programmer builds from a general design toward a more detailed one

    structured design
    QMDWEMWDZI IZQSUB

5. Design that determines the logical order of program instructions

    construct
    EJBQMDWEM

6. Type of control structure that shows one or more actions following each other in order

    sequence
    QZXWZBEZ

7. Type of control structure used when a program performs one or more actions repeatedly

    repetition
    DZCZMSMSJB

8. A language's set of grammar and rules specifying how to write instructions for an algorithm

    syntax
    QPBMHL

9. Design tool that uses a condensed form of English to convey program logic

    pseudocode
    CQZWIJEJIZ

10. Utility that identifies syntax errors and finds logic errors in a program

    debugger
    IZAWUUZD

11. The use of test data to step through the logic of a solution algorithm

    desk check
    IZQF EYZEF

12. Another name for a comment symbol

annotation symbol
HBBJMHMSJB QPGAJV

13. Control structure that repeats one or more times as long as a condition is true

do-while
IJ-RYSVZ

14. Series of steps programmers use to build computer programs

program development cycle
CDJUDHG IZKZVJCGZBM EPEVZ

15. Borland's powerful visual programming tool that is ideal for large-scale development

Delphi
IZVCYS

16. HTML codes that specify links to other documents and how a Web page displays

tags
MHUQ

17. Collects data from visitors to a Web site, who fill in blank fields

processing form
CDJEZQQSBU OJDG

18. Simple, open scripting language that anyone can use without purchasing a license

JavaScript
THKHQEDSCM

19. Web page development language that can be used to define a link to multiple Web sites

eXtensible Markup
ZLMZBQSAVZ GHDFWC

To lure expert programmers, in addition to high salaries and
MJ VWDZ ZLCZDM CDJUDHGGZDQ, SB HIISMSJB MJ YSUY QHVHDSZQ HBI

signing bonuses some companies offer such perks as
QSUBSBU AJBWQZQ QJGZ EJGCHBSZQ JOOZD QWEY CZDFQ HQ

flexible hours, day care, family leave, stock options, workplace
OVZLSAVZ YJWDQ, IHP EHDZ, OHGSVP VZHKZ, QMJEF JCMSJBQ, RJDFCVHEZ

fitness centers, and even laundry service.
OSMBZQQ EZBMZDQ, HBI ZKZB VHWBIDP QZDKSEZ.

DISCOVERING COMPUTERS 2007

STUDY GUIDE

CHAPTER 14

Enterprise Computing

Chapter Overview

This chapter reviews the special computing requirements present in an enterprise-sized organization. Various types of users within an organization require different types of information systems. Large information systems become more valuable when they communicate with each other and offer users a great deal of flexibility in interacting with the information system and other users. The chapter discusses e-retailing and the types of businesses that use e-commerce. Enterprises manage complex hardware, including storage area networks, RAID, and blade servers. Requirements for this enterprise hardware often include high-availability, scalability, and interoperability, which they meet with technologies such as grid and utility computing. The chapter also discusses the backup procedures in a large organization.

Chapter Objectives

After completing this chapter, you should be able to:

- Discuss the special information requirements of an enterprise-sized corporation
- Identify information systems used in the functional units of an enterprise
- List general purpose and integrated information systems used throughout an enterprise
- List types of technologies used throughout an enterprise
- Describe the major types of e-commerce
- Discuss the computer hardware needs and solutions for an enterprise
- Determine why computer backup is important and how it is accomplished
- Discuss the steps in a disaster recovery plan

Chapter Outline

I. What is enterprise computing? [p. 714]

An enterprise refers to _____

_____

Enterprise computing involves _____

_____

Functional units are _____

_____

A. Organizational structure of an enterprise [p. 716]

Supporting activities are _____

_____

Core activities are _____

_____

Operations refer to _____

_____

A decentralized approach to information technology exists when _____

_____

A centralized approach to information technology is _____

_____

B. Levels of users [p. 717]

In an enterprise, users typically fall into one of four categories: executive management, middle management, operational management, and nonmanagement employees.

1. Executive management [p. 718]

Executive management focuses on _____

_____

Strategic decisions center on _____

_____

2. Middle management [p. 718]

Middle management is responsible for _____

_____

Tactical decisions are _____

_____

3. Operational management [p. 718]

Operational management supervises _____

_____

Operational decisions involve _____

_____

4. Nonmanagement employees [p. 718]

Nonmanagement employees include _____

_____

Empowering users means _____

_____

C. How managers use information [p. 718]
Enterprise information is _____

_____

Managers are_____

_____

- Planning involves _____

_____

- Organizing involves _____

_____

- Leading (or directing) involves _____

_____

- Controlling involves _____

_____

Business intelligence (BI) includes _____

_____

Business process management (BPM) includes _____

_____

Business process automation (BPA) provides _____

_____

II. Information systems in the enterprise [p. 720]
An information system is _____

_____

A procedure is _____

_____

A. Information systems within functional units [p. 720]
1. Accounting and finance [p. 721]
Accounting software manages everyday transactions, such as sales and payments to suppliers. Financial software helps managers budget, forecast, and analyze.
2. Human resources [p. 721]
Human resources information systems (HRIS) manage _____

_____

An employee relationship management (ERM) system automates and manages _____

_____

3. Engineering or product development [p. 722]

Computer-aided design (CAD) uses _____

_____

Computer-aided engineering (CAE) uses _____

_____

3-D visualization allows _____

_____

4. Manufacturing [p. 722]

Computer-aided manufacturing (CAM) is _____

_____

Computer-integrated manufacturing (CIM) uses _____

_____

Material Requirements Planning (MRP) is _____

_____

Manufacturing Resource Planning II (MRP II) is _____

_____

5. Marketing [p. 723]

A marketing information system serves as _____

_____

A market research system stores and analyzes data _____

_____

6. Sales [p. 724]

Sales force automation (SFA) software equips _____

_____

7. Distribution [p. 724]

Distribution systems provide _____

_____

8. Customer service [p. 724]

Customer interaction management (CIM) software manages _____

_____

9. Information technology [p. 725]

The information architecture of the company is _____

_____

The chief information officer (CIO) reports _____

_____

Web site management programs allow _____

_____

Security software enables _____

_____

B. General purpose information systems [p. 725]

Enterprise-wide systems are necessary for two reasons:

(1) _____

(2) _____

General purpose information systems generally fall into one of five categories:
office information systems, transaction processing systems, management
information systems, decision support systems, and expert systems.

1. Office information systems [p. 726]

An office information system (OIS), or office automation, is _____

_____

2. Transaction processing systems [p. 726]

A transaction processing system (TPS) is _____

_____

A transaction is _____

_____

Data processing initially referred to _____

_____

Batch processing is _____

_____

Online transaction processing (OLTP) is _____

_____

3. Management information systems [p. 727]

A management information system (MIS) is _____

_____

A detailed report usually lists _____

_____

A summary report consolidates _____

_____

An exception report identifies _____

_____

Exception criteria are _____

_____

4. Decision support systems [p. 728]

   A decision support system (DSS) helps _____

   _____

   An online analytical processing (OLAP) program is _____

   _____

   Internal sources of data can include _____

   _____

   External sources of data can include_____

   _____

   An executive information system (EIS) supports _____

   _____

5. Expert systems [p. 729]

   An expert system is _____

   _____

   A knowledge base is _____

   _____

   Inference rules are _____

   _____

   Artificial intelligence (AI) is _____

   _____

   Knowledge workers are _____

   _____

   Knowledge management (KM) is_____

   _____

   Knowledge management software (KMS) is used to _____

   _____

C. Integrated information systems [p. 730]

   It often is difficult to classify an information system as belonging to only one
   of the five general types of information systems.

   1. Customer relationship management [p. 730]

      Customer relationship management (CRM) systems manage _____

      _____

2. Enterprise resource planning [p. 731]

Enterprise resource planning (ERP) provides _____

_____

3. Content management systems [p. 732]

A content management system (CMS) is _____

_____

Metadata is _____

_____

To index content means _____

_____

III. Enterprise-wide technologies [p. 733]

Several technologies adopted by enterprises allow companies flexibility and the ability to move swiftly in a business environment. By using standard and accepted technologies, the company does not need to reengineer solutions to typical problems.

A. Portals [p. 733]

A portal is _____

_____

Enterprise search technology allows _____

_____

Personalization is _____

_____

B. Data warehouses [p. 734]

A data warehouse is _____

_____

Web farming is _____

_____

A click stream is _____

_____

C. EDI [p. 735]

EDI (electronic data interchange) is _____

_____

D. Extranets [p. 735]

An extranet is _____

_____

E. Web services [p. 735]

Web services include _____

_____

F. Document management systems [p. 736]

A document management system (DMS) is _____

_____

A repository is _____

_____

G. Workflow [p. 736]

A workflow is _____

_____

A workflow application is _____

_____

H. Virtual private network [p. 736]

A virtual private network (VPN) is _____

_____

A VPN tunnel is _____

_____

IV. E-commerce [p. 737]

Several market sectors have taken advantage of business opportunities on the
Web. The more popular market segments include retail, finance, entertainment
and media, travel, and health.

A. E-retailing [p. 737]

E-retail (or e-tail) occurs when _____

_____

B. Finance [p. 738]

Online banking allows _____

_____

Online trading allows _____

_____

C. Travel [p. 739]

A shopping bot is _____

_____

D. Entertainment and media [p. 739]

The technology behind the Web has enabled entertainment and media to take many forms, including music, videos, news, sporting events, and 3-D multiplayer games.

E. Health [p. 739]

Many Web sites provide up-to-date medical, fitness, nutrition, or exercise information. As with any other information on the Web, users should verify the legitimacy of the Web site before relying on its information.

F. Other business services [p. 740]

Some examples of enterprises that use the Web to provide services to customers and other businesses include: _____

_____

_____

V. Enterprise hardware [p. 741]

Enterprise hardware allows _____

_____

Redundancy means _____

_____

The availability of hardware measures _____

_____

A. RAID [p. 741]

A RAID (redundant array of independent disks) is _____

_____

Level 1, called mirroring, is_____

_____

Striping is _____

_____

B. Network attached storage and storage area networks [p. 742]

Network attached storage (NAS), also called a storage appliance, is _____

_____

A storage area network (SAN) is _____

_____

C. Enterprise storage systems [p. 743]

An enterprise storage system is _____

_____

Fibre Channel technology is used to _____

_____

A tape library is _____

_____

A CD-ROM server or DVD-ROM server, also called a CD-ROM jukebox or
DVD-ROM jukebox, holds _____

_____

Internet backup enables _____

_____

Outsourcing is _____

_____

D. Blade servers [p. 744]

Blade servers (or ultradense servers) pack _____

_____

A blade is _____

_____

A blade server chassis can hold _____

_____

E. Thin clients [p. 744]

Thin clients are _____

_____

The personal computer blade is _____

_____

F. High-availability systems [p. 745]

High-availability systems continue _____

_____

Uptime is _____

_____

Downtime is _____

_____

Hot-swapping allows _____

_____

Redundant components allow _____

_____

G. Scalability [p. 745]

Scalability is _____

_____

H. Utility and grid computing [p. 745]

Utility computing (or on demand computing) is _____

_____

Grid computing combines _____

_____

I. Interoperability [p. 746]

Interoperability is _____

_____

Open systems are _____

_____

Closed, or proprietary, systems are_____

_____

VI. Backup procedures [p. 747]

A full (or archival) backup copies _____

_____

A differential backup copies_____

_____

An incremental backup copies _____

_____

A selective (or partial) backup copies _____

_____

Continuous data protection (CDP), or continuous backup, is ___

_____

Backup procedures specify _____

_____

A. Disaster recovery plan [p. 747]

A disaster recovery plan is _____

_____

1. The emergency plan [p. 748]

An emergency plan is _____

_____

2. The backup plan [p. 748]

A backup plan is _____

_____

A hot site is _____

_____

Failover is _____

_____

A cold site is _____

_____

A reciprocal backup relationship is _____

_____

3. The recovery plan [p. 748]
The recovery plan specifies _____

_____

4. The test plan [p. 748]
A disaster recovery test plan contains _____

_____

Self Test

Matching

1. ____ BPM
2. ____ CAE
3. ____ CAM
4. ____ CIM
5. ____ MRP
6. ____ SFA
7. ____ CIO
8. ____ OIS
9. ____ TPS
10. ____ NAS

a. a server placed on a network with the sole purpose of providing storage to users and information systems attached to the network

b. software type that equips traveling salespeople with electronic productivity tools

c. executive position that reports to the CEO

d. includes a set of activities that enterprises perform to optimize their business processes

e. information system that enables employees to perform tasks using computers instead of manually

f. information system that generates accurate, timely, and organized information so managers can make decisions and solve problems

g. the use of computers to control production equipment

h. uses computers to integrate the many different operations of the manufacturing process

i. helps users analyze data and make decisions

j. information system that captures and processes data from day-to-day business activities

k. uses computers to test product designs

l. an approach to information management that uses software to help monitor and control processes related to production

True/False

____ 1. A centralized approach to information systems usually increases costs of maintenance and decreases manageability.

____ 2. Management information systems often are integrated with decision support systems.

____ 3. External sources of data used by a DSS might include sales orders, MRP and MRP II results, inventory records, or financial data from accounting and financial analyses.

_____ 4. Inference rules are the combined subject knowledge and experiences of the human experts in a given field.

_____ 5. It often is difficult to classify an information system as belonging to only one of the five general types of information systems.

_____ 6. Based on a user's actions, a CMS processes content, categorizes the content, indexes the content so it can later be searched, and stores the content.

_____ 7. By using standard and accepted technologies, a company does not need to reengineer solutions to typical problems.

_____ 8. VPN is a set of standards that controls the transfer of business data and information among computers both within and among enterprises.

_____ 9. Several methods are available through which a company can accept payments from a customer.

_____ 10. Blade servers continue running and performing tasks for at least 99 percent of the time.

Multiple Choice

_____ 1. What kind of activities relate to running the business?
     a. supporting
     b. tactical
     c. operational
     d. core

_____ 2. Which kind of decision involves day-to-day activities within the company?
     a. feasibility
     b. technical
     c. tactical
     d. operational

_____ 3. Which of these includes identifying and combining resources so the company can reach its goals and objectives?
     a. planning
     b. controlling
     c. leading
     d. organizing

_____ 4. Which software type often runs on PDAs or notebook computers?
     a. SFA
     b. CAM
     c. CAD
     d. CIM

_____ 5. Which software type manages the day-to-day interactions with customers?
     a. SFA
     b. CIM
     c. CAM
     d. MRP

_____ 6. What were the functions of a TPS initially referred to?
   a. OLTP
   b. data processing
   c. batch processing
   d. automation

_____ 7. Which kind of report identifies data outside of a normal condition?
   a. exception
   b. criteria
   c. identification
   d. transaction

_____ 8. What are programs that analyze data, such as those in a DSS, called?
   a. EIS programs
   b. MRP programs
   c. OLAP programs
   d. AI programs

_____ 9. Which of the following is a special type of DSS that supports the strategic information needs of executive management?
   a. CRM
   b. OLAP
   c. EIS
   d. ERP

_____ 10. What is a group of two or more integrated hard disks called?
   a. NAS
   b. CD-ROM server
   c. RAID
   d. SAN

Fill in the Blanks

1. _____ includes several types of applications and technologies for acquiring, storing, analyzing, and providing access to information to help users make more sound business decisions.

2. _____ systems provide forecasting for inventory control, manage and track shipping of products, and provide information and analysis on inventory in warehouses.

3. A(n) _____ is an individual business activity.

4. A(n) _____ system is an information system that captures and stores the knowledge of human experts and then imitates human reasoning and decision making.

5. _____ is the application of human intelligence to computers.

6. _____ is the process by which an enterprise collects, archives, indexes, and retrieves its knowledge, or resources.

7. _____ provides centralized, integrated software applications to help manage and coordinate the ongoing activities of the functional units of an enterprise, including manufacturing and distribution, accounting, finance, sales, product planning, and human resources.

8. A CMS includes information about the files and data, called

_____.

9. A(n) _____ is a collection of links, content, and services presented on a Web page and designed to guide users to information they are likely to find interesting for their particular job function.

10. A data _____ is a huge database that stores and manages the data required to analyze historical and current transactions.

Complete the Table

VARIOUS BACKUP METHODS

TYPE OF BACKUP	ADVANTAGES	DISADVANTAGES
Full	Fastest recovery method. All files are saved.	_____
Differential	_____ _____ _____	Recovery is time-consuming because the last full backup plus the differential backup are needed.
Incremental	_____ _____ _____ _____	Recovery is most time-consuming because the last full backup and all incremental backups since the last full backup are needed.
_____	Fast backup method. Provides great flexibility.	Difficult to manage individual file backups. Least manageable of all the backup methods.
_____	The only real-time backup. Very fast recovery of data.	Very expensive and requires a great amount of storage.

Things to Think About

1. Should employers use computers to monitor some, or all, office activity? Why or why not?

2. How might companies respond to the problem of former employees downloading customer information from SFA software as they leave the company?

3. Do you make e-retail purchases? What factors influence your decision about whether or not to make a purchase online?

4. What categories of information systems (OIS, TPS, MIS, DSS, and expert systems) would each level in an organization (executive management, middle management, operational management, and nonmanagement) be most likely to use? Why?

Puzzle

Use the given clues to complete the crossword puzzle.

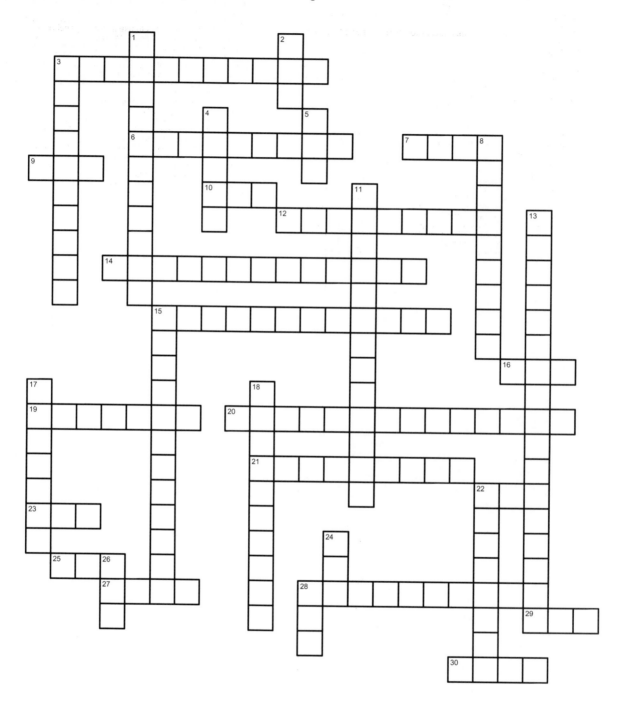

Across

3. Decision involving day-to-day activities within the company
6. Decisions that center on a company's overall goals and objectives
7. Type of activities that involve what the business does
9. Uses computers to test product designs
10. Uses computers to integrate the many different operations of the manufacturing process
12. Type of backup that allows the user to choose specific files to back up
14. Type of employee that includes production, clerical, and staff personnel
15. Systems that provide forecasting for inventory control, manage and track shipping of products, and provide information and analysis on warehouse inventories
16. Uses a computer and special software to aid in product design
19. Person responsible for coordinating and controlling an organization's resources
20. Individual operating entity within an enterprise
21. A set of instructions a user follows to accomplish an activity
22. Information system that captures and processes data for day-to-day business activities
23. Special type of DSS that supports the strategic information needs of executive management
25. An information system that enables employees to perform tasks using computers instead of manually
27. Type of backup sometimes called an archival backup
28. A large organization that requires special computing solutions because of its size and large geographical extent
29. An approach to information management in a manufacturing environment that uses software to help monitor and control processes related to production
30. Programs that analyze data, such as those in a DSS

Down

1. An individual business activity
2. The use of computers to control production equipment
3. The core activities of a business
4. In this type of processing, the computer collects data over time and processes all transactions later as a group
5. Information system that generates accurate, timely, and organized information for managers to use in making decisions
8. Type of report that identifies data outside of a normal condition
11. Approach to IT in which departments and divisions maintain their own information systems
13. A set of hardware, software, data, people, and procedures that works together to produce information
15. Type of backup that only copies those files that have changed since the last full backup
17. To grant access to the information necessary to make decisions previously made by managers
18. Type of activities related to running a business
22. Short-range decisions that apply specific programs and plans necessary to meet the stated objectives
24. High-speed network with the sole purpose of providing storage to other servers to which it is attached
26. Software that equips traveling salespeople with the electronic tools they need to be more productive
28. System that automates and manages much of the communication between employees and a business

Self Test Answers

Matching	**True/False**	**Multiple Choice**	**Fill in the Blanks**
1. *d* [p. 719]	1. *F* [p. 717]	1. *a* [p. 717]	1. *Business intelligence* or *BI* [p. 719]
2. *k* [p. 722]	2. *F* [p. 727]	2. *d* [p. 718]	2. *Distribution* [p. 724]
3. *g* [p. 722]	3. *F* [p. 728]	3. *d* [p. 718]	3. *transaction* [p. 726]
4. *h* [p. 722]	4. *F* [p. 729]	4. *a* [p. 724]	4. *expert* [p. 729]
5. *l* [p. 723]	5. *T* [p. 730]	5. *b* [p. 724]	5. *Artificial intelligence* or *AI* [p. 730]
6. *b* [p. 724]	6. *T* [p. 732]	6. *b* [p. 726]	6. *Knowledge management* or *KM* [p. 730]
7. *c* [p. 725]	7. *T* [p. 733]	7. *a* [p. 728]	7. *Enterprise resource planning* or *ERP* [p. 731]
8. *e* [p. 726]	8. *F* [p. 735]	8. *c* [p. 728]	8. *metadata* [p. 732]
9. *j* [p. 726]	9. *T* [p. 738]	9. *c* [p. 728]	9. *portal* [p. 733]
10. *a* [p. 742]	10. *F* [p. 745]	10. *c* [p. 741]	10. *warehouse* [p. 734]

Complete the Table

VARIOUS BACKUP METHODS

TYPE OF BACKUP	ADVANTAGES	DISADVANTAGES
Full	Fastest recovery method. All files are saved.	*Longest backup time.*
Differential	*Fast backup method. Requires minimal storage space to back up.*	Recovery is time-consuming because the last full backup plus the differential backup are needed.
Incremental	*Fastest backup method. Requires minimal storage space to back up. Only most recent changes saved.*	Recovery is most time-consuming because the last full backup and all incremental backups since the last full backup are needed.
Selective	Fast backup method. Provides great flexibility.	Difficult to manage individual file backups. Least manageable of all the backup methods.
Continuous	The only real-time backup. Very fast recovery of data.	Very expensive and requires a great amount of storage.

Things to Think About

Answers will vary.

Puzzle Answer

DISCOVERING COMPUTERS 2007

STUDY GUIDE

CHAPTER 15
Computer Careers and Certification

Chapter Overview

This chapter discusses the strong demand for computer and IT professionals and presents a variety of available computer-related careers. This chapter also focuses on computer education at trade schools, computer-related majors at colleges and universities, job searches, career development planning, professional organizations, and professional growth. Information about certification preparation, examinations, and resources also is presented. Finally, specific certifications are discussed.

Chapter Objectives

After completing this chapter, you should be able to:

- Describe career opportunities in various segments of the computer industry
- Discuss functions of jobs available in an IT department
- Distinguish between trade schools and colleges
- Differentiate among various computer-related majors for college students

- Identify ways to stay current with changing technology after graduation
- List the benefits of certification for employers, employees, and vendors
- Identify ways to prepare for certification
- List the general areas of IT certification
- Name some specific IT certifications in each certification area

Chapter Outline

I. The computer industry [p. 776]

In today's technology-rich world, a high demand for computer professionals exists. The U.S. Department of Labor's Bureau of Labor Statistics (BLS) reports that more than 20 percent of the fastest growing occupations are in computer-related fields.

II. Careers in the computer industry [p. 778]

Job opportunities in the computer industry generally fall into these areas:

- _____
- _____
- _____
- _____
- _____
- _____
- _____

A. General business and government organizations and their IT departments [p. 778]

In businesses and governmental agencies, the information technology (IT) department employs _____

_____

Employees in the IT department are responsible for _____

_____

Generally, the jobs in an IT department fall into five main areas:
The management group directs _____

_____

The system development and programming group is _____

_____

The technical services group is _____

_____

The operations group operates _____

_____

The training group teaches _____

_____

IT department jobs:
Management

- Chief information officer (CIO)/vice president of IT_____

_____

- Chief security officer (CSO)_____

_____

- E-commerce administrator _____

_____

- Network administrator _____

_____

- Project leader/manager _____

_____

System development and programming
- Application programmer/developer _____

_____

- Computer scientist _____

_____

- Database analyst _____

_____

- Software engineer _____

_____

- Systems analyst _____

_____

- Systems programmer _____

_____

- Technical writer _____

_____

- Technical lead _____

_____

- Web page author _____

_____

Technical services
- Computer forensics specialist _____

_____

- Computer technician _____

_____

- Database administrator _____

_____

- Desktop publisher _____

_____

- Graphic designer/illustrator _____

_____

- Network security specialist _____

_____

- Quality assurance specialist _____

_____

- Security administrator _____

_____

- Web administrator _____

_____

- Web graphic designer _____

_____

- Webmaster _____

_____

Operations
- Computer operator _____

_____

- Data communications analyst _____

_____

Training
- Corporate trainer _____

_____

- Help desk specialist _____

_____

B. Computer equipment field [p. 782]
   The computer equipment field consists of _____

   _____

   Computer equipment manufacturers include: _____

   _____

C. Computer software field [p. 782]
   The computer software field consists of _____

   _____

   Computer software industry positions:
   - Project leader or project manager _____

   _____

   - Programmer _____

   _____

   - Developer _____

   _____

   - Technical lead _____

   _____

- Software engineer _____
  _____

- Computer scientist _____
  _____

Leading software companies include: _____
_____

D. Computer service and repair field [p. 783]
The computer service and repair field provides _____
_____

The functions of a computer technician include _____
_____

E. Computer sales [p. 783]
Computer salespeople must possess _____
_____

F. Computer education and training field [p. 784]
Corporate trainers teach _____
_____

G. IT consulting [p. 784]
An IT consultant provides _____
_____

III. Preparing for a career in the computer industry [p. 785]
To prepare for a career in the computer industry, you must decide on the area in
which you are interested and then obtain education in that field.

A. Attending a trade school [p. 785]
Trade schools (or technical schools, vocation schools, or career colleges) offer
_____
_____

An articulation agreement ensures _____
_____

B. Attending a college or university [p. 786]
Three broad disciplines in higher education produce the majority of entry-
level employees in the computer industry.

1. Major in computer information systems [p. 786]
A computer information systems (CIS) curriculum (or information
technology, or management information systems (MIS), or management

information technology curriculum) teaches _____

_____

2. Major in computer science [p. 786]

A computer science (CS) curriculum (or software engineering curriculum)

_____

_____

3. Major in computer engineering [p. 787]

A computer engineering (CE) curriculum teaches _____

_____

C. Searching for computer-related jobs [p. 787]

Many companies list their job openings, internship opportunities, and career opportunities on their Web sites.

D. Planning for career development [p. 789]

Computer professionals must keep up-to-date on industry trends and technology, develop new skills, and increase recognition among peers. Professional organizations, professional growth and continuing education activities, certification, and computer publications are ways to achieve these objectives.

E. Professional organizations [p. 789]

Two influential professional organizations in the computer industry are:

*   The Association for Computing Machinery (ACM) is _____

    _____

*   The Association of Information Technology Professionals (AITP), formerly called the Data Processing Management Association (DPMA), is

    _____

    _____

Special Interest Groups (SIGs) are _____

_____

A user group is _____

_____

F. Professional growth and continuing education [p. 790]

Workshops, seminars, conferences, conventions, and trade shows provide both general and specific information on computer equipment, software, services, and issues.

The International Consumer Electronics Show (CES) brings _____

_____

G. Computer publications and Web sites [p. 791]

Hundreds of computer industry publications are available. Some, like *COMPUTERWORLD*, *InfoWorld*, *PC Magazine*, and *PC World* cover a wide range of issues, while others are oriented toward a particular topic. Most publications also have Web sites. Another source for information is Web sites that discuss or share opinions, analysis, reviews, or news about technology.

IV. Certification [p. 792]

Certification is _____

_____

Sponsoring organizations are _____

_____

A. Certification benefits [p. 792]

Benefits of certification include:

- _____
- _____
- _____

The Institute for Certification of Computer Professionals (ICCP) defines _____

_____

B. Choosing a certification [p. 794]

Selecting a certification requires careful thought and research. Factors to consider when selecting a certification include:

- _____
- _____
- _____
- _____
- _____
- _____

C. Preparing for certification [p. 794]

Certification training options are available to suit every learning style:

- Self-study   _____

                          _____

                          _____

- Online training   _____
  classes
                          _____

                          _____

- Instructor-led
  training

  _____
  _____

  _____

- Web resources

  _____

  _____

  _____

D. Certification examinations [p. 795]

Authorized testing companies provide most certification exams. Most tests are taken using computers so results are known immediately. Some tests use computerized adaptive testing (CAT), which analyzes _____

_____

Occasionally, a certification requires a hands-on lab test.

V. A guide to certification [p. 796]

Certifications usually are classified based on the computer industry area to which they most closely relate: application software, operating systems, programming, hardware, networking, computer forensics, security, the Internet, and database systems. Some certifications are related to more than one category.

A. Application software certifications [p. 796]

Application software certifications sometimes are called end-user certifications. Popular application software certifications include:

_____

_____

B. Operating system certifications [p. 797]

Popular operating system certifications include:

_____

_____

C. Programmer/developer certifications [p. 797]

Popular programmer/developer certifications include:

_____

_____

D. Hardware certifications [p. 798]

Popular hardware certifications include:

_____

_____

E. Networking certifications [p. 798]

Popular networking certifications include:

_____

_____

F. Computer forensics certifications [p. 799]

Popular computer forensics certifications include:

_____

_____

G. Security certifications [p. 799]

Popular security certifications include:

_____

_____

H. Internet certifications [p. 800]

Popular Internet certifications include:

_____

_____

I. Database system certifications [p. 800]

Popular database certifications include:

_____

_____

Self Test

Matching

1. _____ Vice president of IT/CIO

2. _____ Network administrator

3. _____ Application programmer/ developer

4. _____ Technical writer

5. _____ Systems analyst

6. _____ Systems programmer

7. _____ Data communications analyst

8. _____ Network security specialist

9. _____ Quality assurance specialist

10. _____ Help desk specialist

a. evaluates, installs, and monitors data and/or voice communications equipment and software

b. analyzes user requirements to design and develop new information systems

c. writes the instructions necessary to process data into information

d. installs and maintains LANs; identifies and resolves connectivity issues

e. answers questions about hardware, software, or networking

f. configures routers and firewalls; specifies Web protocols and enterprise technologies

g. installs and maintains operation system software and provides technical support

h. converts the system design into the appropriate computer language

i. copyrighted software provided by an individual or company at no cost

j. works with analysts, programmers, and users to create system documentation and user materials

k. reviews programs and documentation to ensure they meet an organization's standards

l. directs a company's information service and communications functions

True/False

_____ 1. The Information Technology Association of America (ITAA) estimates that the current computer workforce is about 10.5 million workers with an expected increase of about two to three percent per year.

_____ 2. In a typical IT department, the management group is responsible for analyzing, designing, developing, and implementing new information technology and maintaining and improving existing systems.

_____ 3. Computer equipment manufacturers include such companies as Adobe Systems, Novell, Macromedia, and Microsoft.

_____ 4. Companies usually pay sales representatives based on the amount of product they sell.

_____ 5. The current shortage of computer instructors in schools, colleges, and universities is expected to end in the near future as the supply of educators with Ph.D. degrees is increasing as demand decreases.

_____ 6. Trade schools offer programs primarily in the areas of programming, Web development, graphic design, hardware maintenance, networking, and security.

_____ 7. After four years of study in a CIS program, students receive an associate's degree usually with an emphasis in software development, systems analysis and design, or networking.

_____ 8. Computing professionals typically obtain a certification by taking and passing an examination.

_____ 9. Professional organizations, such as the Institute for Certification of Computer Professionals (ICCP), establish standards to raise the competence level for the computer industry.

_____ 10. Most certification tests are in an essay-question format.

Multiple Choice

_____ 1. In a typical IT department, what job title oversees Web site performance and maintains links between a company's Web server and Internet access provider?
  a. Web administrator
  b. Web developer
  c. Web graphic designer
  d. Web programmer

_____ 2. What job title is part of the operations group in a typical IT department?
  a. project manager
  b. data communications analyst
  c. project leader
  d. computer science engineer/software engineer

_____ 3. What job title is *not* part of the technical services group in a typical IT department?
  a. database administrator
  b. desktop publisher
  c. corporate trainer
  d. graphic designer/illustrator

_____ 4. In the computer software industry, what job title writes and tests computer programs?
  a. programmer
  b. project engineer
  c. software engineer
  d. system programmer

_____ 5. What challenging job ideally is suited for individuals who like to troubleshoot and solve problems and have a strong background in electronics?
   a. computer education and training
   b. sales representative
   c. consultant
   d. computer technician

_____ 6. In which of the following programs would students possibly take several high-level math courses, at least two semesters of physics, and several electronic engineering courses?
   a. CIS
   b. CE
   c. CS
   d. all of the above

_____ 7. What benefits are offered by both the ACM (Association for Computing Machinery) and the AITP (Association of Information Technology Professionals)?
   a. workshops, seminars, and conventions
   b. Special Interest Groups (SIGs) that bring together members
   c. programs to help with continuing education needs
   d. all of the above

_____ 8. When preparing for computer certification, which of the following is true?
   a. most people prefer to use a combination of self-study, online training classes, and instructor-led training
   b. most certification programs require academic coursework and are not determined by test results
   c. most professionals have the experience and skill to take a certification exam without preparation
   d. all of the above

_____ 9. The Red Hat Certified Engineer (RHCE) program validates mastery of what operating system?
   a. UNIX
   b. Windows
   c. Linux
   d. all of the above

_____ 10. Which of the following is a hardware certification?
   a. CCNP
   b. A+
   c. CLP
   d. MCSA

Fill in the Blanks

1. An IT _____ must possess strong technical skills in his or her specialized area and must be able to communicate effectively to clients.

2. A(n) _____ ensures that transfers from a community college to a college or university will receive credit for most of the courses already taken.

3. The _____ is a scientific and educational organization dedicated to advancing information technology.

4. The _____, formerly called the Data Processing Management Association (DPMA), is a professional association of programmers, systems analysts, and information processing managers.

5. A(n) _____ is a collection of people with common computer equipment or software interests that meets regularly to share information.

6. The _____, one of the largest technology trade shows in the world, brings together more than 2,400 exhibitors and more than 130,000 attendees.

7. _____ ensures quality and workmanship standards and is one way companies can help to ensure that their workforce remains up-to-date on computers and technology.

8. The _____ organizations of certification programs include computer equipment and software vendors, independent training companies, and professional organizations.

9. A technique known as _____ analyzes a person's responses while taking a certification test.

10. Application software certifications sometimes are called _____ certifications.

Complete the Table

COMPUTER DISCIPLINE DIFFERENCES

_____	Computer Science/ Software Engineering	_____
Practical and application oriented _____	_____ Mathematics and science oriented	Design oriented _____
Understanding how to design and implement information systems	_____ _____ _____	Understanding the fundamental nature of hardware
Degrees include _____	Degrees include B.S., M.S., Ph.D.	Degrees include _____

Things to Think About

1. How is the computer equipment industry similar to and different from the computer software industry? Can a person be successful in one industry without knowledge of the other? Why or why not?

2. Are salaries for job titles in a typical IT department (see Figure 15-3 on pages 780 and 781) commensurate with the education, skills, talent, and experience required? Why or why not?

3. What skills must people in computer education and training, sales, service and repair, and consulting share? What skills are unique to an area?

4. How do employees, employers, customers, and the computer industry benefit from certification? What group benefits most? Why?

Puzzle

All of the words described below appear in the puzzle. Words may be either forward or backward, across, up and down, or diagonal. Circle each word as you find it.

```
S N V E K C T C N N V L I U E Z E K Z R Z P T A D C E U O S
M A R Q S E O E V A Z F Q Y B R G Z I B Q L R D T M C S A T
C K I X I N V W A P Z I Y A O T L C E E C S A R X J X E H F
A D K L C Z S W S P Z S Q Z S A E L E S L A D E W E G C J W
K L V M Z T R K R L O E G S P C F K V C N A E E E L O E V B
C W O P S L A W Y I E J W E E H F S D F B F S N B G J R E L
K S H C Q B A C E C C B K C E F B R O Z G S C I A N X T O L
H U G O Q T S I L A I C E P S K S E D P L E H G D B C I T L
K A F M H R N C U T F Y K U P S Y Y Y A S L O N M U I F H N
E J E P L Y W H S I A Y B K S P A E E R Y J O E I D W I K O
B O O U R T Q F E O U D P M A A G W D C S Z L E N A X C Y I
L N H T L G T J R N Y N Y I U Z L F R O T Z S R I E F A P T
O N D E J V T E G P H H P C Y V D B H C E W Y A S L E T E A
K S X R Y P Q X R R X C E C S C Q N L H M K E W T L W I O Z
X S S O B D L X O O W I I X R I Z S V N S U W T R A L O T I
E S M P O S L O U G T Z I S E O B E V S A K P F A C G N X N
I T E E Z C R J P R M F V D S J M J E S N V V O T I O V F A
C W K R A Z Z A A A K K X W P P A C I W A S B S O N E I P G
C Z F A X P W Z Y M L T X U W T H I U T L V C Y R H H R R R
Y C M T R P S I G M Z G T D Y R I H P W Y L X V J C K V O O
J A Y O E I N X N E J X Z N H Y B C O D S T G L H E Y W J G
Q P Z R U D V W B R H M N Y N K S S M R T R M I S T R Q E N
E V Q N U A V R E T S A M B E W E F T J Z O Q R E W X D C I
L R U G F N A I C I N H C E T R E T U P M O C M C D S T T R
W U C B P O I K L L B E G N V R X I C U D H Z Z O A B C L O
R C V C A E N L O Y C E O U U F T I F X R G G I Y W P H E S
Z T D T H A S V C W P R E T I R W L A C I N H C E T Q K A N
Z Z U M F S L K J K A B Q F S O I U S A S W H U S V N O D O
P O A A C C W F D Z H Y X C H R O V R R S J K M D N P M E P
E T O P G A R T I C U L A T I O N A G R E E M E N T Q C R S
```

Guides design, development, and maintenance tasks

Designs and develops software

Oversees Web site performance

Maintains an organization's Web site

Directs a company's information service and communications functions

Oversees all assigned projects

Performs equipment-related activities

Converts the system design into the appropriate computer language

Works with analysts, programmers, and users to create system documentation

Designs and develops new information systems

Installs, maintains, and repairs hardware

Answers hardware or software questions in person, for example

Academic program that emphasizes the practical aspects of computing

Ensures that student transfers receive credit for courses taken

Academic program that stresses the theoretical side of programming

Academic program that teaches design and development of computer components

Offer programs primarily in the areas of programming and maintenance

Scientific and educational organization dedicated to advancing IT

Collection of people with similar computer equipment or software interests

One of the largest technology trade shows

Ensures a level of competency, skills, or quality in a particular area

Companies that develop and administer certification

Certification that tests technical expertise of setting up and administering the Linux operating system

Certification that tests a user's expertise on Adobe software

Former name of the Association of Information Technology Professionals

Certification that tests basic knowledge of PCs, operating systems, networks, and cabling

Certification that tests knowledge of Novell's networking products

Certification that tests knowledge of Web development, administration, and security

Certification that tests expert level knowledge in areas of internetwork communications, security, routing, and switching

Analyzes a person's responses while he or she is taking a test

Certification that tests basic knowledge of forensics ethics, imaging, examination, collection, and reporting

Certification that tests in-depth knowledge of access control methods, information systems development, cryptography, operations security, physical security, and network and Internet security

Another name for the CIS curriculum

Certification that tests a user's skills solving problems associated with applications that run on Windows XP and the operating system itself

Certification that tests technical expertise in one of several areas including managing and troubleshooting Windows operating systems

Certification that tests knowledge of software development process and tools

Certification that tests basic knowledge of access controls, cryptography, data communications, and malicious code

Certification that tests skills required to use SQL Server 2005 to design or install, manage, and maintain a database system

Self Test Answers

Matching

1. *l* [p. 780]
2. *d* [p. 780]
3. *h* [p. 780]
4. *j* [p. 780]
5. *b* [p. 780]
6. *g* [p. 780]
7. *a* [p. 781]
8. *f* [p. 781]
9. *k* [p. 781]
10. *e* [p. 781]

True/False

1. *T* [p. 776]
2. *F* [p. 778]
3. *F* [p. 782]
4. *T* [p. 784]
5. *F* [p. 784]
6. *T* [p. 785]
7. *F* [p. 786]
8. *T* [p. 792]
9. *T* [p. 793]
10. *F* [p. 795]

Multiple Choice

1. *a* [p. 781]
2. *b* [p. 781]
3. *c* [p. 781]
4. *a* [p. 783]
5. *d* [p. 783]
6. *b* [p. 787]
7. *d* [p. 789]
8. *a* [p. 794]
9. *c* [p. 797]
10. *b* [p. 798]

Fill in the Blanks

1. *consultant* [p. 784]
2. *articulation agreement* [p. 785]
3. *Association for Computing Machinery (ACM)* [p. 789]
4. *Association of Information Technology Professionals (AITP)* [p. 789]
5. *user group* [p. 790]
6. *International Consumer Electronics Show* [p. 790]
7. *Certification* [p. 792]
8. *sponsoring* [p. 792]
9. *computerized adaptive testing (CAT)* [p. 795]
10. *end-user* [p. 796]

Complete the Table

COMPUTER DISCIPLINE DIFFERENCES

Computer Information Systems	**Computer Science/ Software Engineering**	*Computer Engineering*
Practical and application oriented	*Theory oriented*	Design oriented
Business and management oriented	Mathematics and science oriented	*Mathematics and science oriented*
Understanding how to design and implement information systems	*Understanding the fundamental nature of hardware and software*	Understanding the fundamental nature of hardware and electronics
Degrees include *A.A., A.A.S., A.S., B.A., B.S., M.S., Ph.D.*	Degrees include B.S., M.S., Ph.D.	Degrees include *B.S., M.S., Ph.D.*

Things to Think About

Answers will vary.

Puzzle Answer

```
S N V E K C T C N N V L I U E Z E K Z R Z P T A D C E U O S
M A R Q S E O E V A Z F Q Y B R G Z I B Q L R D T M C S A T
C K I X I N V W A P Z I Y A O T L C E E C S A R X J X E H F
A D K L C Z S W S P Z S Q Z S A E L E S L A D E E W E G C J W
K L V M Z T R K R L O E G S P C F K V C N A E E E L O E V B
C W O P S L A W Y I E J W E E H F S D F B F S N B G J R E L
K S H C Q B A C E C C B K C E F B R O Z G S C I A N X T O L
H U G O Q T S I L A I C E P S K S E D P L E H G D B C I I L
K A F M H R N C U T F Y K U P S Y Y Y A S L O N M U F H K N
E J E P L Y W H S I A Y B K S P A E E R Y J O E I D W I K O
B O O U R T Q F E O U D P M A A G W D C S Z L E N A X C A I
L N H T L G T J R N Y N Y I U Z L F R O T Z S R I E F A P T
O N D E J V T E G P H H P C Y V D B H C E W Y A S L E T E A
K S X R Y P Q X R R X C E C S C Q N L H M K E W T L W I O Z
X S S O B D L X O O W I X R I Z S V N S U W T R A L O N X I
E S M P O S L O U G T Z I S E O B E V S A K P F A C G N X N
I T E E Z C R J P R M F V D S J M J E S N V V O T I O V F A
C W K R A Z Z A A A K K X W P P A C I W A S B S O N E I P G
C Z F A X P W Z Y M L T X U W T H I U T L V C Y R H H R R R
Y C M T R P S I G M Z G T D Y R I H P W Y L X V J C K V O O
J A Y O E I N X N E J X Z N H Y B C O D S T G L H E Y W J G
Q P Z R U D V W B R H M N Y N K S S M R T R M I S T R Q E N
E V Q N U A V R E T S A M B E W E F T J Z O Q R E W X D C I
L R U G F N A I C I N H C E T R E T U P M O C M C D S T I R
W U C B P O I K L L B E G N V R X I C U D H Z Z O A B C L O
R C V C A E N L O Y C E O U U F T I F X R G G I Y W P H E S
Z T D T H A S V C W P R E T I R W L A C I N H C E T Q K A N
Z Z U M F S L K J K A B Q F S O I U S A S W H U S V N O D O
P O A A C C W F D Z H Y X C H R O V R R S J K M D N P M E P
E T O P G A R T I C U L A T I O N A G R E E M E N T Q C R S
```

Notes